18/32

Peter H. Mann

Students and books

Routledge and Kegan Paul
London and Boston

First published in 1974
by Routledge & Kegan Paul Ltd
Broadway House, 68–74 Carter Lane,
London EC4V 5EL and
9 Park Street,
Boston, Mass. 02108, USA
Set in Monotype Modern No. 7
and printed in Great Britain by
Willmer Brothers Limited, Birkenhead

ISBN 0 7100 7850 1
Library of Congress Catalog Card No. 74-75856

This book is dedicated to W. Gordon Graham
who encouraged the others

Contents

Preface

This book about undergraduates and books forms part of a
continuing programme which I began in 1967 when I was
encouraged to research into social aspects of book-reading by
Mr Henry Schollick, a director of Basil Blackwell's, the publishing house. As a result of Mr Schollick's initiative I was given
grants for three years by the Booksellers' Association of Great
Britain and Ireland for various studies of books and their
readers, and two books were written on this research, as well
as numerous articles.

When I had completed this research I was strongly encouraged
by Mr W. Gordon Graham, the managing director of McGraw-
Hill in Britain, to extend my research into the field of the use
of books in universities, an aspect of book-reading which I had
commented upon in my theoretical model, but on which I had
not collected any empirical data. Mr Graham was good enough
not only to encourage me with his interest, but also, being a
practical man, to pass the cap round to a number of academic
publishers, and was able to provide me with a useful sum of
money to pay for the research.

Being situated in Sheffield University, which has not only an
excellent library but also an outstanding postgraduate school
of librarianship, I have been very fortunate in finding myself
in a situation where help has been forthcoming from the very
beginning. I was, before the research began, a member of the
university's Library Development Committee (chaired by
Professor W. L. Saunders, director of the Library School) and
after the research began I was co-opted to the Bookshop Liaison
Committee. At all stages of the research I have been helped by
my academic and library colleagues, and the list of those to
whom I am indebted within the university is too long to include
here. I would, however, single out for special mention Mr W. R.
Hitchens, deputy librarian of the university library, without
whose generous and knowledgeable co-operation this research
could never have been undertaken. I have received unstinting
help from both the two main university booksellers in Sheffield

and I would like to acknowledge my debt to Mr Philip Sanderson of A. B. Ward (Bowes and Bowes) of Leavygreave and Mrs J. B. Duffield of Hartley Seed of West Street, which is one of the University Bookshops, Oxford (UBO) groups. Both shops kindly made available to me many reading-lists they had received from academics, and also gave generously of their time in explaining to me the intricacies of academic book-selling. At the analysis stage of the research I was, as always, grateful for the availability of the university's ICL counter-sorter and I thank Mr Peter Linacre of the Registrar's Department for his continuing co-operation. Mrs Margaret Sayles, of my own department, continues to decipher my ever-deteriorating handwriting and yet produce excellent manuscripts and my debt to her is incalculable.

I would conclude these acknowledgments by listing those publishing houses, many of them members of the informal discussion circle known as the American Publishers' Group, who invited me to talk to them about my plans and who then showed their interest by financial support and suggestions, but who never in any way attempted to dictate to me how my research should be designed. The full list is: Addison-Wesley; American University Publishers' Group; Cambridge University Press; William Collins; Chicago University Press; W. H. Freeman; Harper & Row; Holt, Rinehart & Winston; Harcourt, Brace, Jovanovich; D. C. Heath (Europe); International Textbooks; McGraw–Hill; John Murray; Prentice Hall; W. B. Saunders; Van Nostrand Reinhold; and John Wiley.

In research which deals with the relationships between publishers, booksellers, librarians, academics and students, one is working in a field of great complexity, and I fear that this book will contain some errors, no matter how hard I try to eliminate them. For any such faults I, and not my many advisers, am solely to blame.

Chapter 1

The theoretical problem

The research described in later sections of this book stems from a general interest in books and their readers which has led the present writer to carry out a number of studies in the general field of book-reading. It may seem obvious to state that books form an important part in any university education, but over the past few years there has been disquieting evidence that for quite appreciable numbers of university students books certainly do not seem to play as large a role as some academics would like them to play. A number of surveys, to be mentioned later, have shown over a period of years that students seem to spend only about a third of the nominal sum allowed for books in their annual grants. The borrowing of books from libraries has not been illustrated by such a simple proportionate figure, but surveys have shown that, for many students, the library is not a place they frequent as much as might be expected.

This lack of book-buying and of book-borrowing often results in an outright and crude condemnation of the university student as an idle good-for-nothing, scraping through his examinations by means of mugged-up lecture notes and perhaps the odd paperback, and largely spending his local-authority and/or parental grant on beer, cigarettes and old motor-cars—if nothing worse.

This grossly distorted picture of the 'typical' undergraduate (if there be such a creature at all) does scant justice to the many hard-working and conscientious students about whom so little is ever written in the newspapers and magazines, and of whom even less is ever seen on the television screen. At times of student unrest in recent years it has always been the small minority of noisy and violent students who have caught the public's attention, because students who just go to their classes, laboratories and libraries do not make news.

In a similar way it is the small proportion of students who do not work and who do not buy or borrow books who are more

1

newsworthy than the normal workers of the student world. But if impressions tend to highlight the unsatisfactory, what corrective can the facts offer? Unfortunately, there is a scarcity of information about the norms of behaviour so far as the use of books is concerned in the university setting. A small number of studies have been made of student borrowing habits, not surprisingly made by enquiring librarians who want to know what is happening in their institutions. There is less evidence about student book-buying patterns, though the Parry Report[1] was very useful in producing some data on this derived from surveys carried out specially for the Committee in a number of universities. On the guidance given to students by members of the academic staff about what to read and what to buy there is even less to report, and on the liaison between lecturers and libraries or bookshops very little is ever said at all.

This present book is an attempt to put the question of the use of books by students in the university into a wider perspective than has been customary in past studies. The only publication known to the present writer in which anything like the perspective here employed has been used was in a paper given by the university librarian of York to a seminar of university booksellers in 1970,[2] and I am sure he will not be affronted if I say that when it came to producing empirical data for his argument he had to draw upon a rather well-known and well-used set of references, none of which was as up to date as could have been wished.

In this present study the use of books by undergraduates is the focus of the research. I am fully aware that books are used by university members other than undergraduates. Postgraduate research students and academic staff make great demands upon libraries and bookshops, but their problems are rather different from those of the undergraduate. It is the ordinary university 'student' reading for his or her first degree who looms so large in every discussion of the use of books. The reasons for this are many, but important amongst them are the sheer volume of demand upon bookshops and libraries for undergraduate texts and readings; the problems of providing books so as to *get* students to read as much as they should; and the assumption, still widely held by many teachers, that a university is a place where young people will begin a lifelong love-affair with the world of books. Amongst these reasons hard-headed business and sentiment may coincide or clash. For academic publishers, best-seller textbooks are an important source of income; for academic booksellers, the October book sales are the fat to see them through the lean months of the summer—and often several other poor months as well; for the hard-pressed lecturer with an over-large class to teach, the availability of personal copies of a good text chosen by himself for his class is of basic importance. Yet in other circumstances there may be cases of courses where no one textbook is required, where a lecturer firmly believes that a wide-ranging reading-list with no priorities is the best self-discipline for a student, and where library and bookseller will only discover what the students need when the students themselves tell them. There are academics who never give students written reading-lists. There are academics who tell students what to read but never tell the library to provide for these needs. There are academics who refuse to tell bookshops what books the students will need, because bookshops are capitalistic profit-making institutions and some academics are prepared to sacrifice their students' welfare to their own anti-capitalist prejudices.

The web of communication concerning books in the university is a tangled web indeed, and it is because of this tangle that the present research seemed to be worth attempting, even though it was recognized *ab initio* that the whole truth could never be published without giving rise to indignant protests at the least or libel actions at the most. But let it be understood here and now that the case of the professor who for years had never ordered any books for the library other than those he had himself written, and the case of the student in the third-year lecture course who had never had a book recommended to him by his lecturer are real examples, not fictions. This study draws upon many illustrations of problems of communication and lack of communication, not all of which can be fully described without giving offence. But what is sought in this book is a *general* understanding of a widespread problem, and so muck-raking has been put to one side, fascinating though it might be.

The communication network

The starting-point for my consideration of the use of books by undergraduates is the premiss that books are *functional* to an undergraduate education. This means that they play a particular part in the educational process and that they have uses to which they are put by teachers and students. It is therefore important to recognize that, if books are to be used successfully in the educational process, there must be knowledge of them amongst several groups of people, and for that knowledge to be held there must be communication between these groups.

Altogether there are five main groups of people concerned with the circulation of knowledge about books. They are (1) the students (2) the lecturers (3) the librarians (4) the booksellers and (5) the publishers. Although it may be a debatable action, I have reduced the communication network to four groups so as to simplify it, and the publishers are set aside as a special group. The reason for this is that communication between students, lecturers and librarians tends to be mainly with the book retailer rather than the book producer, and if the publisher were included in the diagram below it would result in there being twenty lines of communication rather than the twelve which are already regarded as enough to cope with. However, it should not be thought that I am overlooking the relationship between the publisher and lecturer, the publisher and librarian, and, perhaps most important of all, between publisher and bookseller. All these *are* important and will be commented on. But at this stage it is best to strive for simplicity of presentation, and so a relatively simple diagram (Figure 1) using four corners of a square can represent the four groups of people with whom we are concerned, and the lines of communication which exist, or should exist, between them.

Communication lines

Figure 1 has a charming simplicity which masks the problems that arise when it is applied in reality at a university such as Sheffield, where there are over 600 lecturers, 5,000 under-graduates, 55 different departments, 132 named subjects of study, 39 different libraries, and 2 bookshops. Later pages will deal with reality; at this stage we are concerned with the theoretical ideals which describe what might happen if communication were perfect. It should be noted that the twelve forms of communication are actually six pairs, and that, for example, lecturer and student means communication from

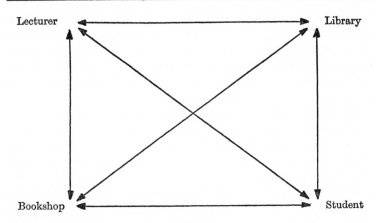

Figure 1   Communication diagram

lecturer *to* student and back from student *to* lecturer. If it is felt that this is a somewhat pedantic point, the answer is that for some staff and students there does seem, *de facto*, to be only the former channel open and not the latter.

When we consider the twelve possible forms of communication, then, they are as follows.

1 and 2: between lecturer and student

It is conventional to regard university lecturers as having a personal responsibility for the lecture courses they give, determining both the form and content themselves and deciding personally what books and other references shall be used in the course. This privilege of personal determination of a course marks off university teaching from school teaching where the syllabus is normally determined largely by the requirements of an external examination board. The university lecturer has both the privilege and responsibility of deciding upon his own syllabus to a large degree. Of course, he is not completely free to do entirely as he wishes, since his head of department, his colleagues, his students and his external examiners will all bring pressure to bear upon him if the actual content of his course bears little relationship to the bare title or short outline contained in a university calendar or faculty prospectus. The lecturer who taught fifteenth-century European history in a course entitled nineteenth-century literature would rapidly be brought to task, though in some academic subjects it may be difficult to decide whether a particular political slant is being given to a lecture course.

Nevertheless, given that the lecturer does determine what he will teach to his students during the forthcoming academic year, it will be expected that the lectures, seminars, tutorials, laboratory classes and so on will be accompanied by a certain amount of reading on the part of the student. Indeed, the traditional form of university study is still referred to by many people as *reading* for a degree. If the student is to organize his work satisfactorily, then it is incumbent upon the lecturer to inform the student what reading is required for the course. This is often done by the circulation, at the beginning of the session, of duplicated reading-lists which will list authors and titles of the appropriate books. In some cases books may be essential to a course, and personal ownership of individual copies by students may be a necessity. In other cases books may be highly recommended for reading but purchase may not be so necessary. The lecturer will have to decide for himself how best his students can be informed about the necessary reading to accompany the course he is to give.

Thus far the problem sounds attractively simple. But in actuality there are many problems to be overcome. In the modern university, and particularly in technological subjects, it is not uncommon for basic courses to be given by a group of lecturers rather than by one person. Indeed, in my own subject of sociology, at Sheffield, departmental policy is now to allow every lecturer to talk on his own speciality to the first-year class, and so, at present, eleven lecturers address these students during the academic year. So the simple example of one lecturer is replaced by 'x' lecturers, and devising a reading-list becomes a group exercise, with all the problems of co-ordination and co-operation.

A further problem of reading-lists is the stage at which a lecturer feels he is prepared to commit himself to a printed list. Although students may expect such a list early in October at the beginning of the academic year, booksellers and librarians need such a list many weeks before this if they are to have the books needed for sale or loan. Such are the problems of acquiring adequate stocks for all university courses in the bookshops that the bookseller must have lists of basic books recommended for *purchase* before the summer term ends, and this is not a time when many lecturers wish to be concerned with such a chore. A further problem of the printed list is that it gives an appearance of committing the course for a whole year to a set of books already published, and really topical books may just be awaiting publication. There is no problem in putting out supplementary lists during the session, but this makes for a rather more fragmented reading-list in the end. Nevertheless, some lecturers do argue that it is better to feed students with references as they go along, and they therefore give only a limited general reading-list at the beginning of the course and supplement this with (usually) verbal recommendations as the lectures proceed. This helps to bring in new publications, but means that the more idle students who miss classes often miss book recommendations, and that the better students who want to read ahead of the lectures cannot do so. There is no simple answer to this problem, though a reasonably detailed initial list with additions as the course progresses does seem to be a working compromise.

Whatever lists are produced, the information process is only completed when students have some ideas about the relative importance of books on the lists. As we shall show later on, some lecturers make careful divisions between basic reading and supplementary reading, and some books may be categorized as A, B, or C, to denote their importance in the course of study.[3] In scientific and technological subjects it is not unusual to have certain books designated as basic to the course, and purchase by students is very strongly recommended. What some publishers of academic books do not seem to understand is that the pattern of usage of books varies tremendously between subjects, and even between years of study within subjects. Most surveys of student spending on books show relatively low spending in the third year, which, stated boldly like this, sounds deplorable. But it may well be that a science student is using journal articles much more than books in this year of study. The problem must be seen in its academic context, and variation of practice between subjects must be recognized.

The line of communication from lecturer to student is clearly of great importance, and, later, empirical data on this matter will illustrate some of the problems to be found. Communication from student to lecturer about books could be regarded as equally important in this theoretical context, since two-way communication establishes a dialogue in place of a monologue. Ideally it could be postulated that the lecturer derives 'feedback' from his students about the worth of the books he recommends, and also suggestions about books which he himself may not be aware of. When books required in the bookshops are not there or if library copies are in short supply, then the lecturer would expect to be informed of these facts by his students. Actuality differs greatly from this ideal pattern, and the line of communication about books from students to lecturers does not appear to be a very actively used one. The result is that, rather than there being an exchange of information and opinion between the two categories of people, there tends to be a line of instructions and directions from lecturer to student with relatively little by way of return. Survey data later will show how little this does happen.

3 and 4: between lecturer and library

Whilst communication between lecturer and student is not between equals, that between lecturer and librarian could be regarded as being between two groups of professionals of equal if different status. The university library has commonly been referred to as the heart of the university[4] and its book collection as one of the fundamental pillars of the whole structure. The content of the book (and periodical) collection will be determined by the needs of the members of the university for both teaching and research, and as the lecturers are those people concerned with these two functions their attitudes towards the library are of fundamental importance. Again, ideally, it could be said that the lecturer will request of the librarian that the library be stocked with those books, periodicals, pamphlets and so on which are necessary for the advancement of knowledge and for its dissemination to students. On his part, the librarian will help the lecturer by providing information about new books and periodicals (which may duplicate information sent direct to the lecturer by publishers, but may often not do so); will arrange for the reasonably quick acquisition and

classification of new books and periodicals; and will so organize
and administer the library that the lecturer is at all times able
to trace references and locate items in the library with a
minimum of difficulty. The librarian also has the important
function of scanning lists of new publications and, if items which
he considers to be of general importance are not requested by
any members of staff, he may himself decide to purchase
certain books because he deems them important for the university as a whole. The functions of the university library are
complex, since it must satisfy the differing current needs of a
variety of people and yet it must provide for posterity as well.
As it was said in the Parry Report:[5]

> The prime obligation of a university library is to the
> members of the institution of which it forms a part. It has
> to satisfy the needs of the undergraduate and must also
> meet the needs of the graduate student who is embarking
> on research and the much more complex and exacting
> demands of the mature scholar.

This is an excellent *general* blueprint for a university library,
although it must be recognized that many individuals, from
the newest student to the most senior professor, may make
virtually no demands upon the library. Nevertheless, the library
must work upon an assumption that demands *will* be made
upon it by a fair proportion of all members of the university.[6]
The functions of the university library will be discussed more
fully in the next chapter, but even at this stage, where we are
considering only the communication network, it is important
to recognize the *information* function of the university library
which is frequently overlooked when a more traditional view
of the university as a *repository* of knowledge is held.[7] For a
university library to function properly it is essential for there
to be constant contact between academic staff and librarians
and, though many of the topics of communication may be
instigated by the lecturer, there is a need for a constant dialogue
between the two groups of people if the library is to do its job.
In the particular circumstances of the provision of reading-
materials for undergraduates, many problems arise of policy
on the provision of textbooks, multiple copies of books, books
available for loan or on restricted use, the provision of an
'undergraduate library' or a 'much-used-book room'. Matters

such as these are of basic importance for the support of undergraduate studies, and it is the undergraduates who suffer (all
too frequently in silence) if the lecturer-librarian communication
channel is inadequately used.

5 and 6: between lecturer and bookshop

In this section we shall include references to the publisher as
well, since his relations with the bookseller are of fundamental
importance to the success of the bookseller's task, and also we
shall consider direct contact between publishers and lecturers,
since this involves a considerable amount of advertising sent
through the post. However, the first consideration must be the
more direct communication between the lecturer and his local
university bookseller or booksellers. With the great increase in
the number of universities in recent years, and particularly
the development of what are now referred to as 'campus'
universities built in open fields adjacent to fairly small towns,
a new type of university bookshop has arisen, which is now
known as the 'campus bookshop' and which is situated in the
heart of the university site on private land, having virtually no
contact with the ordinary town population. This is a strong
contrast to the pattern of Oxford and Cambridge or the older
civic universities developed near the centres of large cities,
where the bookshops serving the universities are commonly
found on main streets in or near the town centre. Peter Stockham has described the problems of university bookselling with
great skill and clarity,[8] and we shall refer in greater detail to
his pamphlet later, but whatever the type or location of the
bookshop may be, its 'bread and butter' is the provision of large
numbers of required and recommended books for undergraduates. Without this trade, university bookselling, which is
a difficult and by no means highly profitable business, would
cease to exist. It is, therefore, of the most fundamental importance that communication between lecturer and bookshop
should be simple, quick and clear. In providing books for
undergraduates, the bookseller is wholly and completely
dependent upon the lecturer for details of his requirements and,
if the students are not to suffer, the communication must be
accurate and early. Here the basic problem of the bookseller
can be seen. The lecturer is concerned with an academic year

which begins early in October and will continue until the end
of the following June or early July. His course of lectures may
be an elementary or very general one, in which the basic books
change little from year to year and in which one or two set texts
may only be ousted after long and careful thought. On the other
hand, he may be giving a very specialized course on his own
research interests to advanced students, and the references he
will use may be very widely scattered amongst periodicals,
monographs, research reports, and small yet expensive books.
In this case, where the content of the *whole* lecture course may
itself not have been determined by the beginning of the session,
the lecturer may be very reluctant to commit himself to a
reading-list for a whole session. In some cases reading-lists for
a term at a time are issued, but booksellers' experience is that
sales of books on the Lent Term lists are never so good as those
on the Michaelmas Term lists.

The decision to 'publish' the reading-list is one which numbers
of academics are reluctant to take until the last possible
moment, and yet the needs of the bookseller are such that, if
he is to have adequate stocks for all students in all subjects, his
communications with publishers must be started in the early
summer, preferably before the long vacation begins in July.
Many academics fail to realize how extremely difficult it is for
booksellers and publishers to provide the correct numbers of
the specified titles without some weeks' (if not months' in some
cases) notice. The extreme example might be a highly specialized
book published by a small university on the west coast of the
USA, which a British lecturer decides he needs for a particular
section of his course. But the lecturer cannot be certain how
many students he may have on his course, since it is an option
decided upon by students at the October registration. He may
therefore tell the bookshop that this book is needed for 'perhaps
between twenty and forty students', which is some guide, even
if a vague one. He may also say that the book will be 'recommended' to the students, which means no more than that they
should *read* it, and that no actual encouragement or direction
to *buy* it will be given. With these instructions, the bookseller
must make his own decision about stocking the book. The
publisher is an obscure university press in a foreign country and
there may not even be an agent for the press in Britain. Orders
must go to the USA; copies (none of which is held in stock

anywhere in Britain or even Europe) must be dispatched from the USA. Multiply this extreme case by many, many other cases of similar or (it is to be hoped) less complexity, and it can be seen why the university bookseller is always asking for time and more time. Even the standard textbooks published in Britain by British publishers can be in the process of revision or a new edition or a new impression, and if thousands of copies are wanted for the beginning of the academic year they must be printed and distributed.

This elementary exposition of the problems of the bookseller and publisher is given here simply because it does seem to me that surprisingly large numbers of academics have no conception whatsoever of the problems of booksellers and publishers, and seem to think that copies of any book can be conjured up by any bookseller overnight. This is not to say that some booksellers and publishers are not inefficient; indeed members of the book trade never cease to agonize over each other's inefficiencies. But it is sad that the relationship between booksellers and publishers and academics is so often a strained one because of the lack of knowledge of each others' problems.

The ideal communication pattern from lecturers to booksellers is, then, one in which the lecturer informs the bookseller as soon as possible what books he will be using in a certain course for a certain number of students. As the bookseller is interested in *selling* books, the list should indicate what books it will be necessary for students to purchase; those that may be strongly recommended for purchase; and others which may be useful to read but not necessarily to buy. The bookseller then has some guide as to the priorities for his own job and can concentrate on getting adequate stocks for the appropriate time. On his part, the lecturer should be informed as speedily as possible if any books are out of print, re-printing, or in any circumstances which might delay their arrival. The usual form of communication from the bookshop to the lecturer is a circular letter sent either to *all* lecturers or (in large universities) to heads of departments during the summer term, and this conventionally asks for titles, authors, publishers if possible, and expected numbers of students. In some cases the bookseller receives departmental lists organized by the head of department or (frequently) one of his senior lecturers. In some universities the bookshops try to establish personal contact with a 'bookshop-

liaison' member of staff who is personally interested in taking
on those duties. Whatever system is used (and a new system
recently adopted at Sheffield is described in Appendix I), it
is important that an efficient channel of communication be
established, with two-way communication between bookseller
and lecturer, otherwise there will be difficulties for the students
in October, and students, lecturers and booksellers are likely
to end up with bad tempers and hard feelings.

The relationship of the publisher to this particular channel
of communication is important, since he is responsible for
seeing that booksellers obtain the correct books ordered, in the
correct numbers, as soon as possible. Errors do occur from time
to time and wrong books or wrong editions are sent to booksellers, and delays in dispatch are one of the most serious
problems of the book trade not yet overcome by co-operative
distribution systems or the use of computers. Apart from the
summer rush, when publishers have to do their best to stock up
the university bookshops, the single-copy orders which go on
all through the year are one of the sorest points, producing deep
rifts between students and lecturers and between booksellers
and publishers. Every academic has his own tale to tell of the
incredible inefficiency of the bookshop in not obtaining the
most ordinary book within three months, six months and so on.
(As I write in July 1973, I am myself still awaiting a British
book first published in 1971 and ordered in October 1971, and
as my need for this book is now not great I shall wait without
reminding my bookseller of the order just to see when, if ever,
it will arrive.) Booksellers are responsible to their customers
for obtaining books not in stock; unfortunately booksellers
cannot control publishers' deliveries, and too frequently
customers are told nothing about their orders as the weeks
go by. For students especially, the textbook ordered in October,
when the bookshop had run out of stock, frequently seems less
and less necessary as they progress through the session without
it. When it does eventually arrive the student may not bother
to collect it, or if he does (perhaps because he had to pay a
deposit on ordering it) he feels aggrieved at the loss of use of
the book because of the delay. In this situation all the people concerned in the transaction have suffered in one way or another.

There is today a considerable amount of direct advertising
of books sent by publishers to university lecturers, and as a

result of this departmental mail in a morning may contain a high proportion of advertising literature. Although much of this goes straight into the waste-paper basket, studies do indicate that lecturers derive some value from being made aware of forthcoming books which *are* in their fields of interest and, since the actual advertising costs are relatively low, publishers tend to devote quite large proportions of their (albeit very small) budgets for advertising academic books to this form. With the advent of the University Mailing Service (now the IBIS—International Book Information Services) in which several publishers banded together to try to reduce 'broadcast' mailings by means of questionnaires completed by lecturers in which their interests were specified, lecturers should, in theory at least, receive less irrelevant advertising. But the IBIS system only operates for a limited number of subscribing publishers, and other houses continue to inundate lecturers with information, not infrequently with two or three copies of the same advertisement in the same post.

The offer of free books in return for recommendations or adoptions for classes is not used on such a scale in Britain as it is in the USA, but it is common for lecturers to be invited to send back postcards asking for inspection copies of books which they may retain (sometimes on a sliding scale of payment according to recommendation) if they so wish. Some publishers are fairly liberal in sending free desk-copies to lecturers, as they believe that a book on the lecturer's desk is a strong incentive to him to use it in his course. This system of direct soliciting has its advantages and disadvantages, though some booksellers express disquiet at the way in which it can come close to direct selling from publisher to lecturer, by-passing altogether the stock-holding retailer. Some academic publishers who have used the system have found themselves badly bitten by lecturers who take a book for nothing, saying that they will recommend it for purchase to a class of, say, twenty students. The publisher informs the local bookseller of this, the book is obtained for stock and then, when the term begins, the book is *not* recommended by the lecturer and both publisher and bookseller have wasted time and money. The academic 'book-grabber' has done much to reduce publishers' enthusiasm for this exercise, and academic publishers appear to be using it with more discretion. The publisher's representative, who calls on lecturers to acquaint them personally about his list and to try to find out what new books lecturers feel are needed, has been cut out altogether by some academic publishing houses, and in other cases is now more cautious about distributing free books. Nevertheless, in some cases the visit of the 'publisher's rep.' (or field editor, as he may be designated on his card) is still regarded by some lecturers as a sort of Father Christmas affair. This rather sordid relationship is not improved when the visiting representatives turn out to be young and inexperienced newcomers to the book trade who clearly know practically nothing about the lecturers' subjects and with whom any sensible discussion about the book-needs of a particular subject can only be at the most elementary level. Experienced representatives are invaluable to the book trade, but novitiate young representatives being 'blooded' on academic staff can be a nuisance.[9]

It could therefore be said that communication between publishers and lecturers is either systematic and impersonal or rather haphazard and not always very satisfactory when the personal touch is attempted. Communications initiated by lecturers with publishers appear to be very limited indeed unless they are concerned with the possibilities of the lecturer being published by a particular house. Publishers do receive a limited amount of correspondence from lecturers, but it would appear to be a very mixed bag, ranging from complaints about excessive prices to enquiries about books long out of print; it rarely seems to be concerned directly with improvements in the provision of books for undergraduates.

7 and 8: between library and student

This channel of communication is one which can greatly exercise the minds of librarians, but which is very difficult to open up successfully. It is important that students should be able to use a library well if they are to derive the full benefits from their university education. In discussions with students it is apparent that the amount of knowledge that students have when they arrive at university varies tremendously. Some who come from schools with good libraries (and, often, keen librarians) may not find it difficult to become *au fait* with how a large and complex library such as a university one operates; but other students whose schools have had poor library facilities can easily be overawed by the university library, which may be one of the largest buildings they have ever worked in.

All university libraries try to give at least basic instruction in the library and its use to the new students, but this instruction is normally only of a voluntary type and not all students attend. Were it not for the practical problems raised by the enormous numbers of students involved and the very limited numbers of library staff available, a good case could be made for compulsory instruction in library use for all new students. Libraries nowadays are trying hard to improve their basic teaching in library use, and film slides, tapes, films and so on are now in use in the universities. But simply to know how to use the general catalogue, how to find a book by the Dewey classification scheme, and how to fill in a borrowing-slip is far from knowing how to use a library for a history essay or a civil-engineering project. Expertise in the *subject* field requires specialized library staff and the interest and support of academic staff.

Many first-year undergraduates take fairly general introductory courses which may use standard textbooks which students should buy. For essay or project work the student may need to find his way round the library shelves, but it is rare for a first-year student to be concerned greatly with abstruse journal articles or specialist research monographs. For the first-year student in arts or social sciences, who is perhaps reading three quite separate subjects, the reading requirements may be adequately met by his own books and a limited number of texts from the departmental or general library. Indeed, for some first-year students it would seem (from examination scripts) that any reading at all is of a very limited nature and does no more than back up the general themes of the lectures they attend.

If the undergraduate course is such that the student has a fairly general first year and then begins to specialize in his second year, this is the time when his knowledge of how to use the library becomes crucial. To take an example from the social-science faculty at Sheffield, all first-year students attend three separate subject courses, usually of three hours' lectures each per week, plus seminars and tutorials. At the end of the first year the students opt for the courses they are to read in their second and third years, and a majority choose to read for a single-subject degree. This degree will consist of ten different courses, a few of which may be examined at the end of the second year, but most of which will be two-year courses examined at the end of the third (and final) year. So the second-year student entering the single-subject school *could* be involved in ten different courses, though in fact the actual figure is more likely to be between six and eight. Nevertheless, he will be moving into reading for specialized topics within the one academic discipline, and the change in book- and journal-needs may be considerable. From the *general* instruction of the first year, perhaps given by a group of lecturers using basic texts, the student now becomes involved in the specialist topics of the lecturers, and the references he will need are likely to become quite sophisticated.

Yet it would appear to be a fairly rare thing for *second*-year students to receive library instruction at the beginning of the academic year, since it is assumed by the teaching staff that they now know their way round the library, and the library staff, who may be more aware of the students' ignorance, must devote their own limited instructional resources to coping with the new influx of first-year students. The need for a greater appreciation of the problem by academic staff and for greater teaching resources in the library is of importance, but my own experience has shown that students must themselves be convinced of the need if this instruction is to succeed.

Three years ago I initiated instruction in library resources for sociologists in their first term of the second year. The visits to the library were to cover general sociological sources, statistical sources, and government publications, in three separate periods. The students were divided into two groups for more personal contact with the librarian. Attendance at the two initial classes was poor and declined so much by the second that the third meeting was abandoned. When I asked some of the better students why the project was so badly supported, there were the usual complaints of it being boring (and some students in this class rarely attended conventional lectures, so they did not turn up for library instruction) but the most startling reason given was that the students had been shown round the library when they were 'freshers' and to be 'shown round' again in their second year made them feel self-conscious and like freshers again.

Since this experience, the library instruction I now organize with the help of the library staff has been greatly changed to make it more of a 'search' project with very practical aims and results. But I was greatly saddened by the earlier reactions of even well-intentioned students who could not appreciate that specialist instruction in their subject was valuable and necessary. Later in the academic year some of the same students who were beginning on dissertations were unable to use some of the simplest bibliographical and search tools of the library, and only then did it dawn on them that there was more to using the library than simply looking for books on the open shelves.

This illustration is used because it shows how difficult it is for the *library* to have successful communication with students, even if there is active support from a member of the academic staff. What is now becoming more generally accepted is that subject-specialists are important in libraries, so that borrowers can turn to library staff who have some knowledge of and sympathy with their problems. The university science library at Nottingham is a good example of a building divided by floor between subjects, with subject-specialist librarians readily accessible to the users.

But every librarian and academic knows that relations between the library and the students are not always so amicable and knowledgeable as they might be. Students who *do* ask for help at the voucher counters frequently find themselves enquiring of young untrained assistants whose knowledge of their subject is virtually nil and who may not even know (as one actual case showed) what departmental libraries exist in the university. As in bookshops, the 'customer's' contact is frequently with the person at the bottom of the hierarchy— the youngest and rawest recruit who knows the least and, sad to say, sometimes cares little, too. Skilled professional advice from the chartered librarian to the undergraduate is an ideal to be sought, but one very difficult to attain. Not every library has always shown a great deal of interest in developing this relationship, though there do seem to be stirrings of change these days. From the student side the demand for a better relationship does not yet appear to have arisen at all.

9 and 10: between library and bookshop

The relation between library and bookshop is perhaps the least considered one in the whole of the theoretical model. Since the library is a part of the university and is thus a non-commercial organization aimed at providing books and periodicals for loan, and since the bookshop is not a part of the university (even though it may be sited on the campus) and is a commercial undertaking which must make a profit from the sale of books or close down, the two institutions are organized in different ways to provide different services for the student. Ideally, the provision of books on loan and books for sale should be seen as complementary services rather than as competing ones, and if the provision of books in all ways for students is to be at the most efficient level, then library and bookshop should each know what the other is doing. Unfortunately, in practice, this is not always so, since both are dependent upon the lecturer for information which is not always forthcoming.

In theory we might say that the basic function of the bookshop is to make available those books which students must or should buy, so that there is no lack of availability to deter the student from purchasing. The function of the library will have to be determined by library purchasing policy, but generally speaking it is usual to agree that the library should not spend a great proportion of its funds on providing multiple copies of books which should be purchased by the students themselves. This is a very important point of principle when dealing with first-year classes of perhaps two hundred or more students, for whom an adequate library supply of basic textbooks for loan could quickly eat up a large amount of the book fund. It is now commonplace for university libraries to provide perhaps half a dozen copies of certain basic books, some of which may be permanently available for use in the library in a reserve-book room, undergraduate library, or much-used-book room. But it can be appreciated that even six copies between two hundred students may well be inadequate if a book is to be referred to constantly. In some departments, especially language departments, funds may be directed to providing multiple copies of texts or commentaries in the departmental libraries, and numbers of twenty or more copies are not unusual. Nevertheless, even with provisions such as these, the language departments normally indicate in their reading-lists that certain books should be purchased, and students are expected to have their own personal copies for use in classes.

The relationship between librarian and bookseller is thus greatly dependent upon the importance attached to ownership of certain basic books by the undergraduates, and this degree of importance can only be decided by the lecturer, who must then communicate his decision to student, library and bookseller. If the lecturer fails in this responsibility, then the student will not have guidance on whether or not to buy; the bookshop will not have guidance on whether or not to stock the book; and the library will not have guidance to help determine how many copies to hold and where to place them.

Even with the best co-operation from lecturers, the information which librarians and booksellers have to work on may not always produce the desired results. A lecturer may say that a particular book is basic to a course, yet the local bookseller may sell copies to only a quarter of the class and be left with many unsold copies in his shop. Even the librarian who provides several copies of the book in the library may find that the amount of borrowing of the book is much smaller than its apparent importance in the course would have indicated. In these cases the explanation may be that students are either using alternative (and perhaps cheaper) books or else, as is not uncommon, they are relying upon a good set of lecture notes to get through the examination.

Generally speaking, the communication between library and bookshop about student book-needs seems to be informal and greatly dependent upon the personal relationships (if any) that develop between the staff of the two organizations. Both bookshop and library do come into regular contact in the process of ordering and supplying books for the university library, and the local bookshop can expect to get some, though not all, of the orders for books which the library is purchasing. This very direct relationship between library and local bookseller is a delicate yet important one, since the library's annual spending on books and periodicals may be well into six figures. Whilst libraries will obviously not want to divulge what amount of trade they actually give to each bookshop, the impression one gains is that the library's purchasing policy is to ensure that the best service is assured whilst still attempting to give a reasonable amount of business to the local shop (or shops) simply because they *are* the local stock-holding booksellers, who should be helped to continue in business because of the other services they provide. If the local bookseller's service to the library does become poor, then this relationship is strained, and the library may well come to feel that it is not its function to support a less efficient local firm if a non-local one is more efficient. The whole relationship is a very delicate one and is made easier if there is regular contact on an easy informal basis between several people in each institution. The bookseller should provide information, on-approval copies, and a rapid order service to meet the library's needs, and this communication will, in the ideal pattern, obviate the misunderstandings and lack of information which so often lead to poor relationships between the two staffs.

Given good personal relationships between booksellers and librarians over the library's own needs, then the two bodies may find it easier to co-operate over problems concerning students. It is by no means always the case that lecturers send their reading-lists to both booksellers and libraries, and informal contacts between the two groups of book-providers can help to overcome this lack of information. In the new Sheffield system, in which lecturers send their student book-recommendations to the library, where they are xeroxed and then passed on to the two university bookshops, a deliberate attempt has been made to place the library in a key position in the communication network, and to ensure that library and bookshop are equally well informed about the lecturers' needs.

11 and 12: between student and bookshop

The relationship between student and bookshop is the most clearly commercial one of all the six depicted by the lines of communication in the theoretical model. The basic function of the bookshop is to supply the student with the books he wants as efficiently and speedily as possible. To do this the bookshop must have a good idea of what the students' needs are so that it can have the appropriate stock in the shop when the term begins. The onus is upon the lecturers, not the students, to tell the bookshop what these book needs are, and so the student with his beginning-of-term reading-list should expect to be able to walk into the bookshop and find the books he wants on the shelves.

In those American campus bookshops which function more

as textbook repositories than actual bookshops, a student may be able to go into the shop and simply ask for those books prescribed for a certain course. Such a system does not operate in any British bookshop I have ever heard of and it is probable that neither British students nor booksellers would care for a system that makes book-buying and book-selling such a thought-less and mechanical process. In Britain the degree of importance attached to any one book still leaves many other books as options, so far as purchase is concerned. This makes life very hard for the bookseller, who may have to decide for himself what stock to get in for a class of (as in one Sheffield case) twelve students with over thirty undifferentiated recommended books on the lecturer's list. The student, though, is rarely aware of the problems of stock-holding in book-selling and for him the bookshop is the place where he expects to find on sale the books he wants. Usually his subject will be displayed in a subject area of the bookshop and it is customary to use a shelf display based mainly on alphabetical order by the authors' surnames. However, so many paperback books are recom-mended today that the student may find himself having to seek a book in the 'Penguin bookshop' area as well, and perhaps in other publishers' special displays. Only the larger bookshops can afford the shelf space to display the same paperbacks in several parts of the shop.

If the student does find the book he wants in stock, there is no great problem, so long as he can afford to pay for it (though an enormous increase in pilfering in recent years indicates the popularity of not paying where this can be avoided). The biggest problem in the student-bookseller relationship is undoubtedly the difficulties that arise when the book the student wants is not in stock and has to be ordered. Sometimes the lack of stock arises from the bookseller having underestimated the likely sales at the beginning of the session and, if things go well, he may be able to drum up extra copies within a few days. But such are the problems of book ordering that I think it is not unfair to say that people who order books do not expect them to arrive within a few days. If there are rival university book-shops in a town, the student may try a second or third shop rather than order from the first, but all booksellers know that, when books are not available from stock early in October, the need for them amongst the students seems to decline as the term progresses, and deliveries to the shop later in the term may well stand unsold.

In certain cases the booksellers do try to keep students informed of the position regarding wanted books not in stock, and small notices saying that a popular text is out of stock and that further copies are expected the following week appear pinned to the shelves. At times this lack of stock *does* arise from a too-timid ordering policy on the part of the bookseller, but this is not always such stupid behaviour as lecturers and students tend to think. After all, a bookseller makes his living from selling books and (even though some lecturers may doubt it) the bookseller does *want* to sell as many books as possible. He knows full well that a book not in stock is often a book which will not be ordered, but equally he works from his own stock-records and tries to be realistic in his stock policy. Books in stock occupy space, and bookshop space is costly. To hold a hundred copies of a law or economics book because there are a hundred students in a class may be the ideal for the student, but if the bookseller knows from his recorded experience that over the past three years he has never sold more than twenty copies a year, he will be a brave, indeed foolish, bookseller to stock many more than that figure. Then, if the book suddenly looms larger in the lectures, or if there is a new tutor who is very keen on the book, demand suddenly rises and the bookseller is caught out. Both students and staff then point to the reading-list which clearly recommends the book, and it is never an acceptable answer for the bookseller to reply that he did not expect so many students to buy the book. Copies may be held on a sale-or-return basis, and most academic publishers are fairly reasonable about returns from bookshops, but even with a liberal returns-policy there are the high costs of transport of unsold books, more accounting to be done, and perhaps dead stock because of a new edition forthcoming. Students cannot be expected to know of all these complexities of the book trade, but it is a great pity that they rarely have any ideas at all of the workings of the book trade and the very slender margins that university bookshops work on: some of them, in fact, actually operate at a loss. This is not to exonerate university bookshops from their responsibilities to provide a service to students which in countless instances is not met with in practice. Students complain, and rightly so, of bookshop assistants who know nothing about government publications and their series numbers, about new editions of well-known standard texts, or about recently announced and well-publicized new books. And when the assistants give an impression that they not only do not know but they also do not care, then the student is confirmed in the view, so commonly held by his lecturers, that the local bookshop is hopeless. Managers and senior staff of university bookshops are only too aware of the problems that arise from the lack of communication between bookshop and student, and in a good bookshop everything is done to ensure that the junior staff are carefully recruited and well trained, since it is the junior staff who are in the closest contact with the customers, and it is on their performance that the shop is judged. A survey of Dillon's University Bookshop made in 1969[10] showed a high degree of satisfaction with the staff there, but Dillon's is one of the largest and best-known university bookshops in the country, and smaller provincial shops cannot hope to provide the service or expertise of a shop of this size with such varied personnel. In the many university bookshops of the provinces good staff are not always easy to recruit, although recent over-production of graduates and increasing unemployment have recently resulted in more choice for booksellers in filling their junior posts.[11] But, even for the most talented young person, bookselling is a very demanding occupation, and university bookshop customers can be difficult in their needs and unsympathetic to the bookshop. This line of communication is not an easy one.

Conclusions

In this chapter the pattern of communication between lecturers, students, librarians and booksellers has been considered in an ideal form. It can be seen from the model and from subsequent commentary that some channels of communication are easier to operate than others and, indeed, a few lines of communication do not seem to operate very much at all.

In studies which have been made in the past of the place of books in the university, the greatest interest has been shown in the provision of books for loan, and most research references are to be found, not surprisingly, in librarianship journals or reports of committees dealing with library problems. University book-selling has received some attention, and references are to be found dealing with its problems in a few librarianship journals, but more commonly in the book-trade periodicals. The whole network of relationships dealt with in the communication model described in this chapter cannot be said to have been covered in any one piece of empirical research, and many studies of borrowing from university libraries ignore the important role of the lecturer in providing basic information about student reading. What is more commonplace in library research is to analyse the use made of library services by students, without enquiring into the guidance they have received from their lecturers and tutors. Since such studies tend to assume that all students are equally well instructed in book needs by their lecturers, it can be seen that this type of analysis begs many questions. Nevertheless, university librarians and special committees of enquiry have done invaluable work in assessing the functions of the university library, and more thoughtful booksellers and publishers have considered carefully their roles in the promotion of books for students. The next chapter surveys work previously done in this field and attempts to draw together some threads from such studies.

Chapter 2

University libraries and bookshops

Introduction

The theoretical model discussed in chapter 1 has not been used for any previous empirical research studies, but this is not to say that all aspects of the model have been completely neglected. There is continuous research being carried out into the use of university libraries, and university book-selling itself has a small literature.

Librarianship is an academic discipline in itself as well as a practical profession, and it should be recognized that many of the problems of university libraries are concerned with questions far wider than simply their use by undergraduates. Indeed, it has been argued that the recent expansion of student numbers has diverted too many library resources to the provision of teaching materials for the transitory student, and that this has led to the neglecting of the libraries' duties to longer-term scholarship and research. In this study we are not able to deal with the broadest issues of university librarianship, and indeed, since the author is a sociologist and not a librarian, he would not claim competence to pronounce on these issues of basic policy. Nevertheless, it is essential to recognize that any consideration of the use and non-use of books by undergraduates is a matter of concern to both librarians and lecturers, and the purchase or non-purchase of books brings together the interests of librarians, lecturers and booksellers. What I have attempted in this chapter is a consideration of some of the main problems of university librarians and booksellers as they are dealt with in publications covering the last twenty years or so, a period which has seen great changes in the basic principles of university education. In selecting from the literature I have tried to choose those publications which have made the most useful references to problems of communication between the four groups of people concerned in the theoretical model. We begin with a survey of problems associated with the university library, and then go on to consider problems of university booksellers. This general discussion may then be regarded as a base from which to move on to the social survey at Sheffield University which is described in subsequent chapters.

University libraries: basic functions

Thomas Carlyle said that 'The true University of these days is a collection of books.' This is a stirring statement indeed, but Carlyle has been dead nearly a hundred years now and his conception of a university is somewhat outdated. The present function of the university library has been cogently described by the Committee on Libraries of the University Grants Committee (the Parry Committee) in the following words. It says of the university library, 'It is a repository for a great variety of material, in manuscript, typewritten, printed, photographed and recorded-speech form, which it is important to preserve irrespective of whether or not it is being put to current use.'[1] In this sentence the Parry Committee sets down the long-term function of the library which must never be lost sight of if the university library is to fulfil its duties to posterity. Then the Committee goes on to describe the social aspects of the university library's functions and it says, 'The prime obligation of a university library is to the members of the institution of which it forms a part. It has to satisfy the needs of undergraduates and must also meet the requirements of the graduate student who is embarking on research and the much more complex and exacting demands of the mature scholar.'[2]

In the above sentences the words 'needs' and 'requirements' raise many questions. The whole Parry Report is concerned with elucidating these needs and requirements, but at the very onset the undergraduate is separated from the postgraduate student and the 'mature scholar', who may be a lecturer, but who is not explicitly referred to in such restricted terms. The important division is between the graduates and scholars who are advancing knowledge and the undergraduates who are still learning about the subject from the senior scholars. The division between research and teaching is thus basic to the thinking of the Parry Committee, and this is in line with most views on the functions of universities themselves and thus of the libraries which are a part of them.

The terms of reference of the Parry Committee give a useful

indication of the practical problems which then arise in trying to obtain the desired levels of performance. The Committee was set up:[3]

> To consider the most effective and economical arrange-
> ments for meeting the needs of universities . . . for
> books and periodicals, taking into account expanding staff
> and student populations, the possible needs of other
> users, the growth of research, the rising cost of books and
> periodicals and the increasing cost of library accom-
> modation; to assess how far greater use might with
> advantage be made of shared facilities, both between the
> institutions themselves and between them, outside library
> systems and other institutions and of modern methods
> of reproduction; and to report.

In these wide-ranging terms of reference there are apparent a number of themes. One is the fairly straightforward problem of coping with larger university institutions and how to give the best services to readers when the numbers of users rise by large proportions. In this the need for branch libraries, multiple copies, reserve-book rooms, undergraduate libraries, and so on are all problems to be considered. A second theme is the need for rationalization of library services in higher education, and the possibility of co-operative schemes between local libraries and even, using new techniques of closed-circuit television and so on, libraries many miles apart. In this way of looking at problems a national, rather than individual, university plan can be envisaged. Already important research on this type of action has been done, and a current major project at Sheffield University Postgraduate School of Librarianship and Informa-tion Science is studying the feasibility of co-operation between the local university, polytechnic, institute of education, and colleges of education.[4]

But in addition to expansion and rationalization, the need for economy is added to the Committee's instructions. Rising costs bedevil all forms of public provision in inflationary times, and it is implicit in the terms of reference that libraries are not to expect higher proportions of money from public funds. The exercise thus calls for professional skills and ingenuity to meet greater demands with, proportionately, no greater resources. If, then, the university libraries are to fulfil their traditional functions even more successfully than they have done in the past, it is necessary to take a long cool look at what *is* happening, so as to plan more skilfully for what might be.

In an article written in a forthright style, a very experienced librarian, L. Jolley, discusses the functions of the university library and states that 'A university is an institution which is engaged in both transmitting and expanding knowledge. The two functions are not distinct. However fashionable it may be to stress the importance of teaching, teaching of a true university character can only be given by those engaged in research'.[5] In putting forward these views, Jolley is reiterating what Bruce Truscot said years before[6] and is upholding the dual nature of the academic's role. With the massive expansion of universities in this country in recent years, there has been a need to recruit staff in disciplines where there have, until very recently, been only slender resources set aside for research studentships. As a result there have been many people recruited to junior staff positions in, for example, the social sciences, who have had only slight research experience and who may well have published nothing even when confirmed in their lectureships. In this way expansion has probably led some young academics to emphasize the needs of teaching to defend their own lack of publication. If Jolley is right and research and teaching should go hand in hand, then clearly, rapid expansion of the teaching function must frequently be made at the expense of the research function.

Jolley also has no illusions about the realities of the library's service and believes that 'To the great majority of users the library is simply the place where you go to get your book and that is all there is to it'.[7] This downright view is an interesting contrast to the Report of the Committee on Australian Universities (which Jolley himself quotes) which declares that:[8]

> The library must be found by the student to be a place
> where he is welcomed and encouraged to pursue a
> personal and independent search for knowledge and
> understanding, where his capacities for independence of
> thought and judgment are enlarged and where above all
> he is treated as a scholar to be provided with peaceful
> and uncrowded conditions conducive to scholarly work.

This highly idealistic blueprint for undergraduate scholarship contrasts increasingly with the rather more realistic comments of the Parry Committee when it says that 'Expansion of universities has meant that some young people are drawn from a social background which has not been conducive to reading and study and new teaching methods have to be devised to meet their needs'.[9] The Australian committee appears to put its faith in the provision of an ideal environment, whilst the British committee would appear to believe that some form of remedial teaching for ill-prepared undergraduates is needed. Jolley, working in Australia, appears to favour the British approach when he comments that 'The professional librarian is constantly astonished to find how ignorant most students and many teachers are of the means of acquiring the knowledge they require'.[10]

Problems of expansion

It has already been shown that university libraries may be expected to change in function both as university populations themselves grow and as the libraries' skills and techniques are developed by research. Whilst sophisticated information-retrieval systems may revolutionize future research work, and television links may eventually result in desk-top access to any library for every lecturer, such wonders are far removed from the second- or even third-year undergraduate who does not know how to use the library catalogue and to whom the word 'bibliography' is virtually meaningless. In this present study we are primarily concerned with the struggling student rather than the sophisticated researcher, but both are denied development if libraries themselves are under-developed institutions.

The University Grants Committee stated that:

> The character and efficiency of a university may be
> gauged by its treatment of its central organ, the library.
> An adequate library is not only the basis for all teaching
> and study; it is also the essential condition of research,
> without which additions cannot be made to the sum
> of human knowledge.

This statement was made in 1921. In 1966, forty-five years later, the Report of the Committee on University Libraries of Oxford University said, 'It is a national disgrace that British

university libraries are so starved of money for books. Indeed
it can be demonstrated that the present state of university
libraries constitutes a national emergency'.[11]

W. L. Saunders, who quotes both the above reports, noted
in 1969 that:[12]

> Currently there are nearly 40 university libraries in the
> USA with over a million volumes, of which 14 have over
> 2 million, 8 over 3 million and 3 over 4 million—with
> Harvard at the top with 8 million. Against this, compare
> the position in Britain, where Oxford and Cambridge
> both have around 3 million volumes, but no other
> university library has as many as one million and the
> great majority cluster around the 300,000–500,000 mark.

The Parry Report gave an average of 365,000 (excluding new
universities) with a range from 800,000 volumes down to
160,000.

Saunders does not add that both Oxford and Cambridge
university libraries are copyright libraries, which receive free
copies of every new book published, whether it be academic
or popular fiction. But he does add further useful information,
which deflates the apologist who would say that the USA is a
wealthy country that can afford such luxuries, when he says
that 'Recent figures showed six out of eleven of Australia's
established universities to be spending more on books and
journals than any British university library other than Oxford
or Cambridge'.[13]

Saunders then goes on to reveal that:

> The average expenditure of British universities on libraries
> is somewhat less than 4 per cent of their total income.
> Parry puts forward 6 per cent as the proportion required
> for minimally effective library support. . . . Parry's
> 6 per cent would mean even in Sheffield an increase in
> library funds of the order of £140,000 p.a. . . . At present
> rates of expenditure it would cost an extra £3¼ million
> a year to step British university library expenditure up to
> 6 per cent.

If 6 per cent should seem a high proportion of income to expend
on libraries, Saunders is able to show that in another developing

commonwealth country, 'Canada's leading 33 universities spend on average 8 per cent of their incomes on their libraries and a total of 40 million dollars a year—that is nearly three times the amount which Britain spends on its 50 university libraries'.[14]

More recently, in 1972, the Publishers' Association produced an analysis of university expenditure on books, which created something of a furore.[15] Using figures for 1968–9 published by the UGC, the Publishers' Association made a number of calculations to show the expenditure from recurrent funds on books and periodicals related to numbers of undergraduates and postgraduates. The main calculation, taking books and periodicals expenditure together and dividing by the total number of all students, resulted in Warwick topping the 'league table' with £32 expenditure per student. Another new university, Lancaster, came second at £26.95, and Dundee was third at £24.55. At the bottom came Heriot-Watt University, spending £2.55 per student; Manchester Institute of Science and Technology with £5.25; and the City University (London) with £9.95 per annum per student. All other institutions spent at least £10 per student, with thirty-six under £20 and fourteen spending £20 or more, and Warwick alone in the £30s. When these figures were discussed in *The Times Higher Education Supplement* there was editorial comment on what appeared to be questionable expenditure on periodicals to the detriment of books (with a special comment on 'the unscrupulous profiteering by some publishers of periodicals') and James Thompson, the librarian of Reading University (£12.50 per student), wrote under the heading 'Overall stinginess of university library budgets'. Amongst his comments was a most interesting statement which deserves full quotation.

What is now happening in this country is that university libraries begin to diminish as research libraries. The servicing of students, in the matter of providing under-graduate textbooks, is so obligatory that it tends not to be much affected. The penury of an academic library shows first in the decreasing acquisition of research materials. More and more noticeably, university libraries will become undergraduate libraries unless this process is halted; and for a university library to be an undergraduate library only is a contradiction of the character of a university institution, namely that it comprises both a teaching function and a research function.

Thompson's comments thus lead us back to the dual function of the university library, to provide for *both* undergraduate and researcher and to keep a balance between the two. If, as Thompson claims, the balance is becoming dangerously tilted away from scholarship towards undergraduate provision, then it is necessary to look in detail into how this arises.

Results of expansion

Whatever may be the views of librarians, lecturers or administrators on the principles involved in university expansion, there is no argument about the fact that expansion of student numbers has taken place. University Grants Committee figures give total numbers as 108,000 in 1960–1, 169,000 in 1965–6, and 228,000 in 1970–1. Numbers of students of these magnitudes have clearly necessitated alterations in university organization, perhaps the most noticeable to academics being the increased sizes of their own departmental staffs and the increasing number of administrative staff to service the departments.

Within the university library the impact of student numbers has been felt in the increasing problems of providing for undergraduate study. One major headache is how to provide adequately for increasingly large classes where over a hundred students are all using the same syllabus and reading-list. Multiple copies of student texts are a drain on library resources and there is uncertainty as to whether such provisions should be made, if students can reasonably be expected to purchase their own textbooks.

Jolley sees increasing size as carrying with it special problems when he writes:[16]

A further problem, which belongs particularly to the larger university, is how to meet adequately, economically and efficiently the library needs of very large first year classes. It seems a tenable proposition that, whilst great collections are always associated with large universities, the actual service to students tends to worsen as a university increases in size. It is certain that this is what

happens unless a very special effort is made by the
university to prevent it.

The Parry Report notes that American universities frequently
provide undergraduate collections with open access and extensive duplication, with one copy to every ten (or even five)
students. This very high provision of multiple copies is interesting, since American students are much more strongly
directed as to what books to buy than are British students.
The Parry Committee recommended that:[17]

> Steps should be taken to ensure that students use the
> element of their grants [1972–3 session, £51] intended
> for book purchase to provide themselves with their
> essential reading. This will relieve the university library
> from the purchase of large numbers of copies of students'
> texts, although the library will still have to undertake
> responsibility for providing those books which students
> cannot be expected to buy. It will obviously be the duty
> of the academic staff to advise the library on those books
> which will need to be duplicated and on those which,
> because students have been advised to get their own
> copies, the library should provide only as reference copies.

This is indeed a nice recommendation; the only problem is that
it deals with a theoretical situation where the library actually
does know what books students cannot be expected to buy;
where academic staff actually *do* advise the library about the
need for duplicate copies; and where students really *are* advised
as to what books to purchase themselves. Were all these things
actually done, librarians, academics and students would find
life much simpler than it is.

SCONUL (the Standing Conference on National and University
Libraries) is stated in the Parry Report to have recommended
expenditure of £3 per student per year to provide for much-
used-book stock.[18] With expenditure per undergraduate ranging
between £2.70 and £38.25 according to the Publishers' Association figures for 1968–9, this would mean proportions ranging
from over 100 per cent down to well below 10 per cent.

The answer to high demand by undergraduates for a limited
range of books has frequently been made in the form of a
reserve-book collection which, with local variations, is custom-
arily a special selection of books which may not be removed

from the library and which may be stocked in multiple copies according to the size of undergraduate classes. Books may be held on permanent reserve or may be put on and taken off reserve as they are needed for essays and so on during the session. Superficially, the reserve-book collection seems to answer many problems, but again Jolley throws cold water on untested theory and claims that:[19]

> Evidence from all over the world shows that many books placed in 'reserve' on the recommendation of teaching staff are never used and that too many of the multiple copies which present so imposing a gesture of concern for student needs collect dust on undisturbed shelves.

In his report on the Library of the University of Western Australia for 1969[20] he instances a closed reserve in which books were given out by library staff on request. Of 1,312 books in this section, 249 were never borrowed and only 389 books were ever used more than ten times in a week in a library open for eighty-seven hours. His own estimate was that only 62 books were really needed on closed reserve. Of 20,050 multiple copies in the general collection, he notes that 2,590 were shown to be very much wanted by students by the fact of their having been stolen. Of the remaining 17,460, only 7,620 had been borrowed ten times in either 1968 or 1969; 9,840 books had not been borrowed as much. Jolley is therefore sceptical about special collections and multiple copies which are not used when provided.

Of course, it must be realized that in many cases a student uses the university library as a work-place or study where he is provided with a table and chair in surroundings where he can work with his own books or simply on his lecture notes. Maurice Line, in his Southampton University survey[21] found that 82 per cent of students used the main library for working with their own books, and several studies have shown that, at any given time, up to half the students in the library may not actually be wanting to use its books. Thus the seating facilities of the university library are extremely important and these need to be met, irrespective of book stock.

The expansion of university student populations brings with it many problems for the library, and Bowyer, writing in 1963, now seems rather dated when he says:[22]

The doctrine that the provision of books for undergraduates is a proper function of a university library is
becoming accepted by university librarians and teaching
staff. [But he goes on to say that] a successful policy for
providing students' books in a British university library
appears to depend, firstly, on agreement as to which
titles the library should buy and which the students should
buy and, secondly, on the calculation of the optimum
book-to-students ratio.

In these two activities the co-operation of the teaching staff is
necessary.

The role of the teaching staff

Whilst, to the outsider, it might seem to be only sensible for
there to be the highest degree of co-operation between lecturers
and librarians in the provision of books for students, in actuality
this co-operation would seem to be a very patchy affair. The
Parry Report comments, 'The first requirement is that library
staff should be advised well in advance of the books prescribed
for the courses of the following session. Much greater co-
operation is needed between library and academic staff'.[23] It
then goes on to say that:[24]

Although some measure of cooperation exists between
academics and library staff in some institutions, more
should be done to make cooperation a matter of course.
Returns to our questionnaire showed that in every
discipline except that of law, most members of staff
compiled their prescribed book-lists without any consultation with library staff.

There can be little doubt that many academic staff would be
amazed if it were suggested to them that they should consult
the library staff before compiling their reading-lists, since the
library staff are frequently regarded as book-providers rather
than as professional equals (or even superiors). But the Parry
Committee backs up its principle by pointing out that:[25]

The methods of acquiring students' books in the right
quantity at the time they are required are, of course,
dependent on the closest liaison of the academic staff with

the library staff. It has been known for tutors to recommend books for their students which are not available in
any of the university or other libraries in the vicinity.
We have also heard of books recommended to students
which were out of print and unobtainable on the second-
hand market. This situation would not have arisen if
the library staff had been consulted beforehand. It is
important that reading lists should be checked before they
are issued to students to ensure that the library has, or
can obtain in good time, the items recommended.

If this counsel were followed by all lecturers, there would
undoubtedly be a great improvement in the provision of books,
but it would require lecturers to compile their lists earlier than
they do, in order to allow for consultation and checking, and
also it would require them to treat librarians as equals. Neither
of these requirements is likely to be met without great changes
of behaviour amongst those many lecturers who simply do not
understand what libraries and librarians can do.

Co-operation between lecturers and librarians could obviously
result in a better provision of books, but this would still not
remedy a further problem, which is the overloading of reading-
lists. In his library report for 1969 Jolley[26] says, 'There is a
widespread conviction that reading lists are not as well prepared
as they could be', and he refers to a letter from R. S. Hoare in
the *Library Association Record* which, dealing with the relationship between unrealistic demands and book-thefts asks, 'Is it
better to gear courses to limited numbers of books or extracts
to which students can be guaranteed access, or to recommend
a long list of books in spite of the knowledge that the sheer
physical and administrative effort involved will frustrate many
students from obtaining most of them?' Jolley also refers to a
paper on 'The Australian student: admission, selection and
progress' by Mitchell and Cohen who say 'It would be an
interesting exercise for a Professor . . . to calculate how long
it would take to read (allowing where necessary for the slow
pace required for a first reading with understanding) and reread
all the books which have been listed for a year's course.' These
same writers take the point even further and question the whole
structure of modern undergraduate courses:

For the student, learning in the university is becoming

increasingly a desperate race against time to absorb a certain amount of information. There is not enough time for reflection, discussion, further individual exploration by reading, independent reasoning. Are we already at the stage where we are saying that the purpose of a university education is to teach the student to learn and to think and to evaluate independently and then designing courses of study which, in their demands on their time, make these impossible?

Perhaps he is too sweeping in his claim to know everyone's opinion, but Jolley himself argues that 'Everyone agrees that having failed to raise educational standards by increasing the amount taught it is time to try raising standards by decreasing the amount taught.'

It would be difficult to find many lecturers prepared to teach 'less', though clearly all courses are in a constant process of revision as new knowledge is acquired, and probably what Jolley is aiming his criticism at is the syllabus which forever adds new items but does not discard. This is probably seen best in reading-lists which become so long that there must be problems for students, not only in doing the reading, but also in obtaining the references. The Parry Report makes reference[27] to the School of Social Studies at Sussex University where, in the 1963–4 session, there were 109 references in urban sociology, 111 in American economic history, 141 in political sociology, 190 in British economic history, and so on. Without knowing the full details of the courses and the importance attached to various references, it would be unfair to say definitely that students were being overloaded by their lecturers, but certainly this writer has seen enough reading-lists to know that, when all the separate course reading-lists for a year are put together, the student has an impossible task. The largest reading-list I have ever seen for one lecture course in sociology was from a northern university, where students were given eighteen duplicated foolscap pages of references for the one course, with just over 100 items starred as being 'basic reading'.

It can always be argued that, with very large introductory classes and limited numbers of copies of books available in the library, a wide range of alternative references should be given.

This, however, smacks of expediency rather than principle, and neglects the desirability of students actually buying basic books for themselves. Obviously the mass provision of relatively elementary references for students raises many problems, but it would seem at present that this problem has been seriously considered by librarians only, and not by lecturers.

The students themselves, who are at the receiving end of the reading-lists and are the potential library users, have been surprisingly quiet about these problems, and whilst there has been a certain amount of criticism of forms of teaching and even of syllabuses, comments from radical students on library provisions are difficult to find—even though some of these radical students must be library users themselves. However, there have been a number of studies made of student use of library facilities and some of their findings will now be discussed.

Students in the library

The forms of use made of libraries by students can vary greatly, and it is not easy to impress a simple set of categories of use on to the activities that take place in libraries. The research studies carried out into student use of university libraries are unco-ordinated, and questions asked need only vary slightly from survey to survey to make comparisons impossible. What follows in this section is a general picture of the patterns of use by students, with data drawn from surveys as examples whenever possible.

One may begin by assuming that all undergraduates are library users but (as the Sheffield survey will show in detail) this is a highly unwarranted assumption. In his 1964 study, Humphreys[28] at Birmingham showed that 12 per cent of arts students, 11 per cent of science students, and 5 per cent of commerce students did not *borrow* from the *main* university library, though they could be seat occupiers of it and might well use *departmental* libraries for their needs. In his 1961 survey at Leeds, Tucker[29] reported that 23 per cent of students had not borrowed from university libraries during their student career, however long or short. These varied from 36 per cent in science and 35 per cent in technology to only 11 per cent in arts. Only 8 per cent were not 'readers', that is, users of any sort.

All surveys which distinguish between subjects show differences in library use between arts, science and technology students, and Bowyer, using Birmingham findings, puts forward the tentative generalization that 'It seems that in the Science faculty undergraduate book use tends to be intensive, whilst in the Arts faculty, and possibly even more in the Commerce and Social Science faculty, it tends to be extensive'.[30] This intensive/extensive viewpoint will later be shown to reflect the forms which teaching takes in different subjects, but it should be noted here that for the scientist or technologist with a thirty-hour teaching week the use, if any, of a library must be intensive, compared to that of an arts or social-science student with only a twelve-hour teaching week. Also the need for a range of books varies greatly between courses, and it is accepted that even an elementary course in history uses far more references than a course in, say, civil engineering. Page and Tucker's early survey in Leeds[31] of all borrowings in 1957 showed average borrowings of 17·89 volumes in arts, 10·76 in science and 8·87 in technology. The subject differences in book use have thus been recognized for many years.

An important library-use survey was carried out for the Parry Committee in 1965 by Marplan, a market research firm. Between 17 May and 30 June 1965, 1,383 students at eleven large, ten small and two new universities were interviewed, with samples drawn to include arts, social sciences, pure science and applied science. The universities of Oxford and Cambridge were deliberately excluded, as their library structure makes them atypical. The Marplan survey found that 14 per cent of undergraduates had never used the *main* library, and most of these were applied-science students.[32] This may be significant, but it would be necessary to know how many of the applied-science students had a major branch library for themselves quite separate from the *main* library, as is the case in Sheffield.

When questioned about their knowledge of their libraries, 23 per cent said they found the library layout difficult.[33] Twenty-eight per cent did not know whether or not their main library had a subject catalogue, and 22 per cent did not know if it had an author catalogue.[34] Thus over a fifth of the students were ignorant of what might be called the basic elementary tool for finding books. When asked about their knowledge of bibliographical aids, 33 per cent knew of indexing journals and 37 per cent knew of abstracting journals, leaving about two-thirds who were unaware of these sources. Fifty-nine per cent had heard of the inter-library loan service and 21 per cent had used it, although 24 per cent of those who had used it thought it unsatisfactory, mainly because of delays in obtaining their requests.[35] Approximately half the students said that they never asked for books which were out on loan to be reserved for them (though this figure ranged widely between universities, from 11 per cent to 84 per cent).[36] Fifty-nine per cent had asked for help from library staff at one time or another, but 21 per cent of the users of main libraries said they were reluctant to put queries to members of the library staff, and this was a particular feature amongst first-year students.[37]

In preparing work for academic projects, 39 per cent of the students said they had received no advice as to what to read, and 30 per cent had not used a library for their most recent project; 63 per cent had used source material other than borrowed books for their most recent project—predominantly students' own textbooks or lecture notes. Thirty-eight per cent said that, on the whole, they had found it difficult to obtain in time the books which they needed for their studies.[38] This problem was greater in the humanities than in the pure sciences or applied sciences, and public libraries were often used in an attempt to overcome such problems. However, complaints by students of the lack of books are by no means always justified, and the report gives an example of one case where Maitland's *Equity* was said to be unavailable, when the library actually held ten copies. Nevertheless, it can be seen that, if students do not know how to find books in the library, their chances of not finding them are obviously quite high. Durey notes in his 1968 study at Keele[39] that out of a sample of 389, 93 people, who failed to find material they sought, reported thirty-two items as completely untraceable. On investigation it was found that seventeen of these thirty-two items were not in stock—which presumably means that the other fifteen were in stock.

When asked, in the Marplan survey, about the main problems of a loan system, 31 per cent of respondents said there were too few standard books; 13 per cent commented on problems of people not returning books; and 9 per cent remarked on the period of loan being too short.[40]

The above details from the Marplan survey have been given

because they clearly indicate that things are not right with student borrowers. Too few students know how to use a library properly, and as a result of their ignorance libraries are misused, unused or abused. The lack of skill in using the library is brought out in a survey in 1964 at Birmingham University library, in which undergraduates who had failed to find items they were looking for were classified according to the search procedures they had used. All of them had looked on the library shelves, but only 20 per cent had used the catalogue, and only 8 per cent had asked the library staff for help. Of 189 undergraduates who had visited the library to locate items or topics already known, 92 per cent went to the shelves first and 65 per cent looked on the shelves *only*.[41]

Tucker, in his 1961 survey at Leeds,[42] found that 40 per cent of students used the author catalogue; 17 per cent the subject catalogue; and 11 per cent asked the staff for help. Durey at Keele[43] in 1968 found 44 per cent, 6 per cent and 22 per cent in these three categories. Tucker also found that 35 per cent of arts students said they had reserved books, compared to 39 per cent of science students and 25 per cent of technology students. But a check against the records showed that, in reality, the figures were 27 per cent of arts, 27 per cent of science, and 15 per cent of technology—thus demonstrating that the survey responses exaggerated the number of minority users of reservation services.[44]

Lack of seating for private work which may not require the borrowing of library material is a serious problem in over-crowded universities, and frequently local authority public library reading-rooms are used by students unable to find a place in the university. The Parry Committee reports a memorandum from the city libraries of Birmingham, Bristol, Glasgow, Leeds, Liverpool and Sheffield who said that 'Accommodation in the reference libraries is frequently over-taxed by the number of students wanting seating accommodation'.[45] Line found that 48 per cent of Southampton students used the public library,[46] and Tucker at Leeds had 33 per cent who used 'non-university' libraries for reading or working on the premises.[47] It would be an over-simplification to infer that this usage of public libraries is merely the result of gross overcrowding of university libraries, since surveys of *departmental* libraries show that they are frequently considerably under-used. Whilst there are no data on this phenomenon, one interesting hypothesis is that some students do not like working in the university atmosphere and, for reasons as yet unplumbed, find themselves more at ease in the public library away from the university. An investigation of these students could be sociologically and psychologically interesting.

A further point rarely considered is the exchange of books amongst students themselves. Tucker at Leeds found that 64 per cent of students had borrowed books from other people.[48] There is no evidence in any survey of 'group buying' by students in order to reduce purchase costs and collect a small class library for themselves; certainly attempts to encourage this made by the present writer in past years have never met with any response at all. Since Line found at Southampton that 60 per cent of students said that they 'often' found that a book they wanted was not on the library shelves,[49] it is perhaps mildly surprising that students have not formed any inter-loan co-operatives.

How students use the library

There is general agreement in all studies of students' behaviour in libraries that they tend to look for information (books and periodicals) on the shelves, rather than through catalogues and reference works, and that they are reluctant to ask for advice from library staff. Maurice Line, one of the pioneer surveyors of library behaviour in Britain, gave a very clear picture of how higher-education students go about their work, in a survey of five teacher-training colleges, published in 1965.[50] Line began by classifying borrowers into those who borrowed 'a good deal' (two to three books a week or more); those whose borrowing was 'moderate', and those who borrowed 'rarely or never'. A very interesting point was that older students borrowed considerably more than did the younger ones, taking 'older' as those aged twenty-six or more on entry to the colleges. The overall figures (in percentages) were:

	Good deal	Moderate	Rarely or never
All students	26·3	67·6	6·1

But those aged over twenty-six had 46·7 per cent in the 'good deal' category, those aged twenty-one to twenty-five had 32·4 per cent; and those up to twenty had 22·7 per cent. This age-correlation with library borrowing is one indication of the immaturity in reading of the younger students.

Line found that 22·8 per cent of students never used the catalogue if they could avoid it, and only 5·7 per cent considered it as a *first* resort. He commented, 'Students do not generally use the catalogue if they can help it. They go first to the shelves for the books they want and are therefore greatly dependent on the physical arrangement of the library and the classification'.[51] One question put to students in these five colleges and to Southampton University students asked them, 'Have you ever wanted to find out what material the library has on a definite topic new to you? If you have tried, how did you set about it?' Several methods were listed and the results with college and university percentages are given here:

	University	College
Searching the shelves	66·9	90·6
Classified catalogue	78·0	58·5
Library staff	30·5	63·5
Teaching staff	30·5	41·8
Bibliographies	27·1	31·4

The above categories added together exceed 100 per cent, since all students could be expected to use all methods, and if they all used all the methods every category would be 100 per cent. What is interesting here is the *negative* implications; for example, that 22 per cent of university students and 41·5 per cent of college students do *not* use the catalogue; that 69·5 per cent of university students do not ask the library staff or teaching staff, and so on. This lack of sophistication in search methods obviously must produce poor results when 'look and see' is so popular.

Line went on to question the college students about their reluctance to ask the library staff for help, and of three reasons offered in his questionnaire the first (64·6 per cent) was that students felt their query was too elementary and that they ought to know the answer themselves; the second reason (52 per cent) was that the staff appeared to be too busy to have time to deal with them. Only 22 per cent thought the staff would not be able to help. It had never occurred to 32·3 per cent of students that the library staff could help them with a specialist query.

This survey of Line's, whilst it is in teacher-training colleges rather than universities, nevertheless points very forcibly to the lack of student expertise in using their libraries, and to their lack of initiative in getting appropriate people to help them.

In his survey at Southampton University, Line found that 13 per cent of students never used catalogues if they could avoid it, and 14 per cent said they found catalogues difficult to use. Sixty-five per cent of students said they found library staff helpful, but 39 per cent were reluctant to put queries to library staff, and 51 per cent said it had never occurred to them that library staff could help with a subject query. Nineteen per cent of students had found the library 'intimidating' when they first came up to university and 48 per cent had found it 'mildly intimidating'.[52]

Line's surveys give a picture of students coming to university with little knowledge of how to use a library, being intimidated to some degree by the size and complexity of a university library (or even a teacher-training college library), and not knowing how, or being willing, to use the basic catalogues or the library staff themselves. Line's conclusion was that 'Many of the minor complaints and frustrations are due to a lack of understanding on the students' part and a failure on the library's part to put itself across. The difficulty is to find a suitable channel of communication between the library and the students'.[53] This conclusion is indeed an important one, since the question is so rarely raised as to what channel of communication *can* be developed between university libraries and students. The presence of students on a university library committee itself will not solve this, even if the students do turn up to the meetings. What is clearly needed is *personal* contact between students and library staff as individuals and this can only be brought about by a complete recasting of teaching-staff thought on the use of books. What is needed is education for library use, strongly supported by the teaching staff.

The need for library education

The survey carried out for the Parry Committee by Marplan

found that 75 per cent of the undergraduates interviewed claimed to have used their secondary school libraries for working in, but only 40 per cent said they had been taught how to use these libraries. Thirty-nine per cent claimed that they had received no training in the use of their university library, and of the 61 per cent who had received instruction, 55 per cent had received instruction by a printed document, and 52 per cent from library staff (a slight overlap allows for instruction from both sources). Nearly a third of the 61 per cent who had received instruction expressed the view that it was not very useful.[54]

Enough has been said to show that students are lacking in library skills. Jolley's comments on the implications of this lack of skills are worth recording. He says:[55]

> In a university library the first object of all technical devices must be to provide instruments which will not only enable the student to find his way amongst books and prompt him to discover methods of judging their standing, but will contantly encourage him to extend the range of his interests. It was long ago pointed out that the self-educated man has a very ignorant person for his teacher and the difficulty with all self-service institutions is that the customer too often becomes content with a quite inadequate standard of service. Far too many users of a library never get from it more than a small proportion of what it has to offer.

Jolley then goes on to describe the educational function of the library.

> The real task of the librarian, which is also one of the main tasks of the university, is to train the student to train himself. To achieve this end the librarian has to introduce the student to the library. This is not something which is done once and for all in orientation week. It is a continuous process which may well last the whole of the student's lifetime, and which becomes more obviously valuable the longer it is carried out. For it is true that a library must be known before it becomes clear that it is worth knowing.

In 1965 Line wrote that 'It is now becoming accepted that

some form of instruction in library use is desirable for students
in higher education'.[56] Saunders, in his inaugural lecture to
the University of Sheffield on being elected to its new Chair of
Librarianship said, 'I would personally like to see a much
greater emphasis on the library's teaching role; I see no reason
why a university library, actively involved in the teaching
process, should not be a part of a faculty, carrying out teaching
in all departments of the university, with proficiency in using
books and libraries a required element in every student's
course'.[57] Saunders's hopes are being fulfilled here and there
in scattered experiments in the universities, but as yet it is fair
to say that the principle of library education has probably not
even entered the minds of most university lecturers. No one
would expect a scientist or technologist to work successfully in
a laboratory without some instruction in the use of his equipment, but instruction in how to use 'that on-line, real-time,
random access storage device, the book' (as Saunders so beauti-
fully describes it) is yet in its infancy.

Bookshops, basic functions and problems

Whilst university libraries may rightly be expected to have
stocks of undergraduate books for loan to students, it is also
expected that students will buy books for themselves so as to
have a personal library at hand whenever needed. To this end
the current (1972–3) awards scheme of the Department of
Education and Science, which allows £445 for each student
in higher education living away from home (£480 at Oxford
or Cambridge Universities and all higher-education colleges or
universities in London), suggests £51 for books, equipment and
materials.[58] Students are thus expected to spend about a ninth
of their total income on books etc., and, if their needs are to be
adequately met, good university books are required. The Parry
Report makes a rather curious recommendation when it says,
'It is certain that the existence of a good bookshop on the site
does encourage book-buying habits among students and we
recommend that every institution should ensure that there is a
good bookshop on or near the campus'.[59] Whilst this recommendation is based on common sense rather than empirical
evidence, one does wonder what a university is expected to *do*
to ensure a *good* bookshop on or near the campus. In the case

of new universities on virgin sites at a distance from towns, the customary practice is to provide an empty shop for book-selling and then to invite tenders from recognized booksellers to provide the service. Usually the offer is taken up by an established book-selling group rather than by an individual entrepreneur.

In his pamphlet on university book-selling, Peter Stockham, the managing director of Dillon's University Bookshop in London, explains the problems of university book-selling and shows, especially in the case of campus universities with students in residence for only thirty weeks a year, how very difficult is this type of book-selling. He explains that 'profit margins in university bookselling are not as large as in general book-selling'.[60] This is due to a number of factors, amongst which lower discounts from academic publishers play a prominent part. Although the whole question of discounts is under constant discussion, it could be said, in the most general terms, that for many years 'academic' books have had a discount of about 20 per cent, compared with 'general' books with a discount of about one-third. The reasons for this are partly historical and partly based on arguments of keeping down overall academic book prices, coupled with a supposedly more easily gauged demand. Whatever the rationality or irrationality which lies behind the arguments, 'academic book' discounts are usually lower for the bookseller. Coupled with this, he also has to cater for a demand for books which is most unevenly spread over the year. The general bookseller has a Christmas rush, as do most shopkeepers, but the university bookseller has a mad rush in October, with long periods in vacations and the summer when his sales may be very low. Yet the university bookshop must be equipped with many reference books and bibliographical tools so as to provide rapid and accurate information for its customers. This, in turn, requires skilled specialist staff who *should* be well paid[61] (though book-selling rates of pay in general would make a miner or docker faint) and, as it is located conveniently for the university trade, the shop may often be poorly situated for general book-selling. Stockham considers that 'the university bookseller's greatest difficulty is that of finding suitable staff', but further data may indicate that lack of a proper level of demand for his books is really the basic problem.

University book-selling is a complicated and difficult retail business and, whilst it is not possible to give detailed figures, I have been assured by the chairman of one book-selling group that several university bookshops are barely economically viable and, were they not members of a group, their past losses in certain trading years would probably have led to their closure. Few if any academics or students appear to be aware of these problems, since they themselves are usually lacking in any commercial experience or understanding.

Julian Blackwell explained in simple language the extreme complexity of university bookselling in the *ASLIB Proceedings* in 1962.[62] First he showed that the common supposition held by some purchasers that booksellers are unnecessary middlemen is a facile view. There are (or were in 1962) about 300,000 books in print, any one of which a customer has a right to expect to be able to obtain. The current handbook of 'publishers' gave 1,600 addresses, of which only 380 were full members of the Publishers' Association. Even these numbers do not include many institutions, associations and individuals who from time to time publish reports and monographs for sale. The genuine university bookseller expects to be asked to obtain the most varied types of publications, some of which may well be sold at a *loss* to him, since research institutions and university departments who publish reports frequently do not give a discount to the bookseller. This explains why, in some instances, university booksellers do suggest to customers that they themselves write directly to publishers for rather obscure publications.

Blackwell compared the 300,000 books in print which booksellers must be able to supply with the possible stock of Marks and Spencer, who have between three and four times the volume of the home book trade. Marks and Spencer, he estimated, sold about 500 different articles, which, allowing for differences in colours and sizes, probably amounted to about 5,000 items. Also, no Marks and Spencer store will ever order any item for a customer. The gramophone record industry is often compared (usually favourably) with the book trade, but Blackwell estimated in 1962 that there were only 26,000 different records 'in print'.

He then went on to illustrate the complexity of the work at the internationally famous shop of Blackwell's in Oxford, and analysed one day's orders. There were 3,198 items from forty-three countries. Excluding periodicals, music, second-hand, American and other foreign items, this left 2,786 books published by British publishers to be obtained. Of these Blackwell's, a very big bookshop, had 1,188 in stock already. The remaining 1,598 had to be ordered from 246 different publishers, of which 37 were not included in the above-mentioned list of publishers and their addresses. There were 192 orders for items which were 'not yet published', 141 items were binding, reprinting or out of stock, and 180 items were out of print.

This case study of a day's work at one of the largest bookshops in the country is a splendid example of the intricacy and detail which a university bookseller must expect to cope with every working day, and it must clearly indicate to even the most inexperienced customer how much work the bookseller must contribute in searching for items, and how all this work, often skilled and time-consuming, adds to his overheads.

In addition to the difficulties of sorting out orders, Blackwell notes how difficult are deliveries in the book trade, and he comments that 'We regularly get books from Berlin more quickly than from London.' He notes that some large publishers are suffering badly from computeritis (and even now, ten years later, this disease has not been fully stamped out).

The university bookshop is in a peculiar position in so far as stock is concerned. Comparison between university bookshops in Britain and the USA is here useful. I recall that, two years ago, when a visiting American student who was taking my second-year course received my fairly detailed reading-list, she told me that had this been at her own university near New York she would simply have gone into her 'college book-store', asked for the appropriate required books for 'Dr Mann's course in methods of social investigation' (probably referred to by its code number rather than title), and would have been handed a set of books already parcelled for her. As yet British universities have not reduced either their courses or their bookselling to this level and, as Stockham comments, 'A bookshop is not a publishing warehouse.' He goes on to say:[63]

Stock selection is the most important single task in a bookshop, for it is by his stock that a bookseller will be judged and this is particularly true of a university bookshop. He (the bookseller) must have the books which the staff and the students want, at the time when they want them, and in the right numbers.

Stockham suggests that, of the 26,000 titles produced in one year (now about 30,000 in 1973), probably 'only about five hundred will be books which the university bookseller wants to carry in his stock'. But even so, five hundred *new* items each year is a large number, and demands expert choice on the bookseller's part. How he makes his choice must be dependent largely upon the information he receives from university teachers and students.

Booksellers, staff and students

Stockham avers that 'The customer is the most important person in the bookshop', and he adds that any assistant who does not take an interest in his customers should not be in a bookshop. But he does add that 'The academic customer can sometimes be inconsiderate himself'.[64]

Certainly university lecturers are frequently highly critical of bookshop service, and students, in a less sophisticated way, not uncommonly complain of poor bookshop facilities. It is the latter problem—of the students wanting to obtain fairly straightforward course-books—which raises the biggest difficulties, since student books are needed in large numbers at particular times. Obtaining specialist books for teacher-researchers *is* a problem, but not one about which much is ever written. Blackwell puts the bookseller's case very reasonably when he writes:[65]

Whatever educational responsibility we may accept towards the undergraduates, there can be no doubt that our efficiency as simple purveyors of a required commodity would increase greatly if only we had more cooperation from the universities. We are sincerely grateful to all those departmental heads and lecturers who do provide us with advance copies of their reading lists, but there are far too few of them.

Blackwell's statesmanlike comment is considerably milder than that of the Parry Committee, which reports on discussions with both the National Union of Students and academic staff. The NUS claimed that any failure on the part of students to buy more books was due to two main causes. First:[66]

> Students needed much more guidance from academic staff as to the books they really would require. Sometimes the lists given were exceedingly long and the students had no means of knowing the relative importance of the books listed. When any advice was given it was often contradictory, since members of the same department frequently recommended different books. The students believed guidance to be the joint responsibility of academic and library staff and that it should extend even to telling them about the cheapest available editions.

The main cause was the financial problem of student grants and this will be discussed later.

Replies to enquiries made of academic staff by the Parry Committee showed that:[67]

> Some departments of science, engineering and medicine did not provide reading lists at all to students and of those that did, many gave no priority indications. By far the greater proportion of departments had compiled their lists without any consultation with library staff and there were several departments which gave only occasional advice to students as to which books to purchase from their grants. . . . Academic staff should both encourage students to buy books and give them more specific guidance.

Stockham, from his considerable experience in university book-selling, stresses the importance of the role of the individual lecturer in this encouragement. 'His alone is the persuasion that will cause many a student to go out and buy a book. Enthusiasm for a book on the part of a lecturer can often be infectious and can lead to a quite unexpected level of demand in the bookshop.' He goes further and says:[68]

> The degree of a lecturer's ability to explain to students the reasons for possessing a book and to communicate infectious enthusiasm for the experience of reading it is an indication of the number of students who will read

the book. The lecturer is by far the best person to contact, and it is often futile to rely on the extensive lists which departments prepare for background reading, without knowing who has made out the list and whether the books on it will ever be talked about or used at all. Heads of departments can often help here, for they know how the teaching is delegated and who are the best people to approach about particular subjects.

I would disagree with Stockham to some extent in his belief that heads of departments can always help; frequently the administrative work of a department which concerns the organization of teaching and any co-ordination of reading-lists is done by an experienced senior non-professorial member of staff rather than by the head of department himself. In general, however, Stockham's commentary is admirable and does point to the necessity for *personal* knowledge within the communication network.

Book-buying by students

A matter for considerable dispute over the years has been the actual amount of book-buying by undergraduates, which has always been shown to be less than half that expected by the education ministry when composing the annual student grant. The basic position is set out in the Parry Report, where it is explained that Section I of the 1962 Education Act obliged local authorities to pay a maintenance grant to higher-education students under certain stipulated conditions. 'This grant was to allow for various elements of a student's average term-time expenditure and, although this was not expressly stipulated in the act, was to include an annual allowance of £30 for books, instruments and materials'.[69] Over the years since then, the books etc. component has gradually risen as grants themselves have been raised. In 1965 it went up to £35, and the present position is that student total grants for 1971–2, 1972–3 and 1973–4 have been laid down with small increases each year, giving the student £48, £51, and £54 for books, equipment and materials in each of these years.

It is not the place here to discuss whether the total grants are adequate. Nevertheless it can easily be seen that if students are unable to meet the demands of lodgings and food from the present (1972–3) £240 component, then the present £51 component for books is likely to be 'raided'.

Even though it could be argued that the present time of galloping inflation is perhaps not the best one for considering expenditure on books, past surveys over a period of years have all shown considerable underspending by students on books. Tucker's 1961 survey at Leeds gave an annual average expenditure of £10.50 per student.[70] Line's five-college survey at Southampton in 1965 (when the book grant was £30) gave a mean expenditure of £6.80 and a median of £4.80. Three-quarters of the students spent under £10 and only 4.6 per cent over £21.[71] His 1963 survey at the University of Southampton found that 7 per cent of students had bought no books during the session and the average *numbers* of books claimed to have been bought were, by faculties, 20 in arts, 10 in economics, 8 in law, 7 in science and 6 in engineering. In all faculties there was a decline from first year to third year in the numbers of books bought.[72]

The Marplan survey carried out in 1965 for the Parry Committee at twenty-three universities said that 'the average student had acquired [*sic*] 10·92 books in the course of the academic year.'[73] In the first year the average was 14·56 books with 2 per cent of students having acquired none, whilst in the third year the average was 6·22 books with 10 per cent acquiring none. Overall, the average for arts students was 19·5 books and for applied-science students 7·00 books. There were also wide variations between universities, with averages of 20·08 and 20·33 at two new universities and 6·27 and 7·67 at two older universities. The average expenditure on books per student was between £10 and £11, with much the highest average expenditure in the first year and a steady drop to final year. An interesting further point of detail was that 55 per cent of students claimed that the books they had bought accounted 'for more than half those which they had needed' and this was claimed more by science students than by students of the humanities.

Comparison of British book-buying with American patterns is difficult, since colleges in the USA tend to have a much more clearly directed system of priorities in student books. Nevertheless, it is interesting to find that the report of a large survey in 1971, covering 1,025 students in thirty-six colleges, carried out for the College Division of the Association of American Publishers[74] gave an average spending of $72.12 on books so far during that *semester*, in a survey completed by 29 October. Seventy-six per cent of all students actually purchased the basic textbooks in all the courses in which they were required during what is called 'book rush'. Those who did not do this tended to be in the humanities and social sciences rather than the scientific or technological disciplines. The American system of explicit instructions about what to buy may not recommend itself to British academics, but it clearly does result in American students actually purchasing their own textbooks, and this happens in a system where students do not receive standard grants with a book component.

The general underspending on books by British students has been a topic for consideration for many years, and several reports have commented on it. Bowyer records that in 'University Development 1947 to 1952' the University Grants Committee reported that 'Students now tend to buy far fewer books than they did in the past', and in its review for 1952–7 the Committee stated that 'The modern undergraduate buys fewer books and depends more on libraries than his predecessor'.[75]

Devices to ensure that students do spend on books that component of their grant intended for books have been considered over the years, and a voucher system has been suggested a number of times. This was considered by a committee of the Ministry of Education and Scottish Education Committee under the chairmanship of Sir Colin Anderson, which in 1960 published a report on grants to students. The Anderson Committee advised against book vouchers or similar schemes on the grounds that:[76]

> All the devices for tying the payment are open to abuse
> and, anyway, students commonly buy most of their books
> second-hand. One over-riding reason is, however, that
> the student should be treated as a responsible person and
> left free to spend the money given to him according to
> his own circumstances and his own judgment of his needs.

There is no evidence to support the Anderson Committee's belief that students commonly buy most of their books second-

E

hand, and any survey data would tend to disprove this. As for treating students as responsible people, the critics of this view would argue that, as the evidence over many years has indicated great underspending, students have shown themselves for years not to be acting responsibly in this matter and steps should be taken to remedy this mis-spending of public money which now amounts to several million pounds a year. The Standing Committee on National and University Libraries recommended to the Parry Committee that a system of book vouchers should replace the book element in the grant. The National Union of Students in its submission was particularly concerned that the book allowance was tied to the general grant which, they felt, was then inadequate for general living expenses and so students who had to pay well above the level of the accommodation component of the grant simply could not afford to spend the full book component on books. However, the Parry Report did go on to say

> We understand from their representatives that the N.U.S. would not be opposed in principle to any scheme which would ensure that students did in fact spend their book allowance on books, provided that only a part of the grant was tied to the purchase of prescribed books so that the remainder could be spent at the students' discretion on books of their own choice.

This acceptance by the NUS of direct control over book expenditure is a considerable concession to the principle that, whatever other costs have to be met, book expenditure should not be reduced. If the NUS plea were accepted, then the book component of the annual student grant would be put to one side quite separate from the rest of the grant, and when students could show that the accommodation component was inadequate, as it is claimed to be in 1973, there would be no question whatsoever of robbing Peter to pay Paul.

The Parry Committee, after careful consideration of the differing views held on book purchasing by students, came to the following conclusions: [77]

> We feel very strongly that students must spend their book allowance on books, and it is clear that many of them are buying far too few even when they have grants to

enable them to do so. It is therefore vital that steps be
taken to ensure that the money is properly spent.
We urge that immediate consideration be given to a
voucher system with suitable safeguards. Since no statutory
obligation is imposed on L.E.A.s to allocate a specific
sum of money for books, we realise that our recommendation may involve a new statutory instrument. Since the
administration of a voucher system would be immensely
complex, it might be thought advisable to invite a
commercial firm accustomed to this field to undertake
the planning and administration of the machinery.

The actual working out of a voucher scheme would undoubtedly
have to be undertaken with both tact and professional skill,
but the latter could undoubtedly be provided by Book Tokens
Ltd, a firm wholly owned by the Booksellers' Association of
Great Britain and Ireland, which has now run a most successful
and highly profitable general book-voucher scheme for many
years.

Conclusions

As this review of past discussions on student book-borrowing
and book-buying has shown, the situation is a complicated one,
and for a full and sensible understanding many factors must be
related to each other. The situation should not simply be one
of praising or blaming groups of people: rather it should be seen
as a complex situation involving many groups of people at all
sorts of different levels, where a lack of understanding of the
structure may well be resulting in a lack of knowledge—and
thus a lack of appreciation of what is and what is not happening.
As the theoretical communication-model showed, there are four
main groups of people who should, in varying ways, be in
communication with each other. If they are not communicating,
then the structure is almost certain not to function properly.

To study such a structure empirically over the whole country,
at all the universities in Britain, would be a mammoth task,
and even if it were attempted at, say, a dozen institutions, the
problems of co-ordination and staffing would result in a cost
of many thousands of pounds. The subsequent chapters of this
book give a single case study for one university, carried out

without any research staff at a cost of a couple of hundred pounds. I hope that the low cost of this study will not deter the reader, since it is my personal view that current expenditure on social research projects is ludicrously high for the results produced. The present study has the advantage of being a one-man-job carried out within a period of two years. It is in many ways a participant study, since I have been a member of staff at Sheffield University since 1954 and I have seen the institution grow from about 2,500 students to its present 6,000. During this time a new library has been built; teaching departments have grown and occupied new buildings. The university bookshops have grown in size, and one has moved to new premises. The degree syllabuses have changed enormously, and new departments and faculties have been created. All these changes have had their effects upon the use of books in this university and it would be difficult for a person from outside the university to understand the complex structure that has arisen, within which the use of books takes place. The survey which follows, then, is based upon experience over nearly twenty years; participant observation by a senior member of the academic staff; and a formal questionnaire survey of undergraduates to give statistical data.

The next section, therefore, deals with the structure of the University of Sheffield, which it is necessary to describe before one can go on to deal with the functions of books within the structure.

Chapter 3

Sheffield University and books

Introduction

In this chapter a detailed description will be given of the structure of Sheffield University and this will lead to an explanation of the research study on the use of books carried out amongst staff and students, libraries and bookshops.

Although the University of Sheffield is one of many universities in Great Britain, it is also a unique institution. The uniqueness is particularly important in Britain since, in spite of control by the State exercised through the University Grants Committee, universities in this country are still independent institutions registered as charities. All universities must receive a royal charter before they become officially recognized, and major changes in their statutes must be passed by the Privy Council; but in spite of these formal requirements the universities retain a high degree of autonomy in deciding their own academic policies and syllabuses. As a result of this, universities differ from each other in many ways. Sometimes the differences may be easily apparent, such as a collegiate structure at Oxford or Cambridge compared with a unitary structure at many other universities. Less easily comprehended differences may lie in the internal academic structure, where some universities have a strong departmental basis for degrees, whilst others have schools of studies more important than departments.

Sheffield University is probably as good an example of an 'average' university as any other in the country. It began as a university college in 1897 by the amalgamation of three existing institutions: a medical school, a technical school and Firth College (a higher technical institution). In 1905 the college was granted a charter and became a full university with 100 full-time students. After the First World War, numbers rose to over 1,000 but then stabilized at about 750 in the inter-war years. After the Second World War, numbers again rose and by 1947 the university had 1,700 students. Table 3.1 gives detailed figures for more recent years.[1]

Table 3.1   Full-time students by academic year

Faculty or Department	1955–6	1960–1	1965–6	1970–1	1971–2
Arts	680	750	805	915	900
Law	13	75	214	255	271
Pure Science	548	828	1,239	1,588	1,546
Medicine (incl. Dentistry)	445	501	551	584	637
Engineering	274	563	773	822	832
Metallurgy (Materials Technology)	120	173	296	299	309
Department of Social Studies	17	—	—	—	—
Social Sciences (Faculty)	—	119	610	984	970
Architectural Studies (Faculty)	—	—	186	245	277
Postgraduate School of Librarianship	—	—	33	44	—
Institute of Education	—	—	—	8	8
Educational Studies (Faculty)	—	—	—	—	256
Total students	2,097	3,009	4,707	5,744	6,006
Reading for bachelor degrees	1,639	2,249	3,887	4,696	4,862

Commentary on Table 3.1 will help in understanding the university and its development over the past seventeen years, which has been greatly affected by changes in general higher education policy and especially by the Robbins Report on higher education.

As can be seen, in 1955–6 the university had just over 2,000 students in six faculties and a (then) non-faculty Department of Social Studies which did not give degree courses. The Faculty of Law was comically small at that time and was simply a law department which, by a combination of historical chance and design, had become a faculty in itself. By 1960–1 the university had grown by almost 50 per cent, and a Faculty of Social Sciences (originally titled Economic and Social Studies) had been created, which included the Department of Social Studies and took over existing subjects such as economics, accountancy, politics and economic history, and made them founder-subjects of the new faculty. In terms of student numbers, therefore, this new faculty originally consisted mainly of transfers from the Faculty of Arts. The combined growth of these two faculties between 1960 and 1965 can be seen to exceed that of the Faculty of Pure Science. By 1965–6 another new faculty, that of Architectural Studies, had been created, most of whose students had previously been in the Faculty of Arts. In the five years between 1960–1 and 1965–6 the university again increased in size by over 50 per cent, and in the ten-year period had thus more than doubled its student numbers. By 1970–1 another thousand students had been added, and in the 1971–2 session the Faculty of Educational Studies was instituted, which took in students from the Postgraduate School of Librarianship and Information Science and students in the University reading for the postgraduate certificate in education; it also took over certain other complicated responsibilities for the Institute of Education and local colleges of education. So by 1971–2, the session of the survey of the use of books, Sheffield University had just over 6,000 students in nine faculties, with 4,862 of them reading for first (bachelor) degrees.

The distribution of students in different faculties represents the compromises worked out between UGC suggestions about appropriate development and the university's own wishes. In recent years the pressure from outside, backed by control of grants, has favoured expansion in the arts and social sciences, which are cheaper and easier to expand than the sciences and technologies. The present structure at Sheffield may not be exactly what the senate or council would have chosen, given a free hand, but the balance between faculties has produced an interesting mixture of subjects which belies any stereotype which people may have of Sheffield as a primarily technological university. The Faculty of Metallurgy, which changed to become the Faculty of Materials Technology, covers glass technology, ceramics, polymer technology and materials technology as well as metallurgy; with only 309 students in 6,006, this means that roughly only 5 per cent of the student population is in this faculty, and so any image of Sheffield as a 'steel' university is quite wrong. If the Faculty of Medicine is left to one side, the remaining faculties could be said to give a reasonable balance between humanities and sciences. Arts, Law, Social Sciences, Architecture, and Education have 2,582 students, whilst Pure Science, Engineering and Materials Technology have 2,687. There are many more students reading for higher degrees in the science and technology faculties (504) than in the humanities (203), but, again, this pattern must be common to all universities, since studentships are greatly dependent upon national research grant-giving bodies.

The numbers of full-time members of the academic staff also rose during the period noted above. In 1955 there were 287. By 1960 this number had gone up to 414, and by 1965 it was 618. In 1970 there were 782 and in 1971 the figure was 844. It can thus be seen that the staff-student ratio became generally less favourable for a time, giving figures of 7·3 for 1955, 7·3 for 1960, 7·6 for 1965, 7·3 for 1970, and 7·1 for 1971. Of course, the ratio varied considerably between departments, and at the period of the most rapid expansion in the 1960s there were individual departments with a ratio of 1 staff to 12 students.

The degree structure

A university is an extremely complicated organization, not only because of the large numbers of people involved in it but also because of the wide variety of activities it is engaged in. This present study is mainly concerned with the university's teaching function, but it is essential to note the importance of the research function which occupies so much of the staff's time and is the reason for having twenty-two non-teaching weeks in the year, and teaching duties usually not in excess of ten or twelve hours a week. Teaching duties do vary, however, from subject to subject and this is not surprising when one considers the wide variety of subjects offered in the university. In the nine faculties of Sheffield University there are (according to my personal count, since no official figure is given) fifty-five separate departments, excluding many specialities in the medical school which are hospital based, and 132 different subjects of study.

Departmental staff (full-time teaching only) range from four in music to thirty-four in chemistry, though the latter department has a further twenty-two research workers and research fellows listed in the Calendar. There are many research personnel in the university who do a little teaching, and the medical school particularly has large numbers of part-time staff, usually hospital doctors in the National Health Service who give clinical teaching. All together the full-time teaching staff, plus part-timers and research workers, administrative and library staff adds up to approximately a thousand people.

Students reading for first degrees do so within the faculty structure, since the faculty board is the body responsible, in the first place, for degree syllabuses and examining. However, the degree which the student reads for is possibly one of the most complicated problems to understand in the whole university and it is this complexity which, it is feared, many publishers and booksellers fail to comprehend.

For example, the Arts Faculty may be thought of by the outsider as that faculty within which students read for degrees in English, history, classics, languages and so on. But the situation is not so simple as this. All arts students, in their first year, read three separate subjects from a list of twenty-five different subjects which includes both pure mathematics and applied mathematics, architecture, economics, psychology, and political theory and institutions. Clearly there is a wide range of choice open to the student to read outside the conventional arts subjects. Of course, a student wishing to read for a degree in, say, French, will be required to read French in his first year. In each of Greek, Italian, Russian and Spanish there are two first-year courses, one for beginners and one for more advanced students. The possible permutations of first-year courses for the 307 new students in arts in October 1971 were thus very considerable.

Having passed the examination at the end of the first year, the successful student then enters a particular school of the faculty, in which he spends the next two years reading for his final examinations and B.A. degree. Depending upon the three subjects which he read in his first year and the quality of his work over that year, he may then enter a single school (and concentrate on one subject), a dual school, or a three-subject school. The Faculty of Arts offers fifteen single schools, sixty-seven dual schools and two triple-subject schools, a total of seventy-four different schools for 307 students to choose from. Of course, many students do in fact choose the more traditional schools such as the single schools of English, French, German and so on, but there are on offer interesting combinations such as Greek and Russian, biblical studies and German, and music and philosophy.

In the Faculty of Social Sciences, as in the Faculty of Arts, the first-year student reads three separate subjects, this time from a given list of fifteen subjects plus 'any one modern foreign language offered by the Faculty of Arts', which would seem to encompass the five subjects of French, German, Italian, Russian and Spanish, since Japanese is specifically named in the prior list of fifteen subjects, as its 'home' is in the Social Sciences Faculty. In addition to the twenty subjects so far described, however, the student may also read 'any other First Year subject offered in the University (with the approval of the Head of the Department and the Dean of the Faculty)'. At a rough count this would open up possibilities of just over a hundred other courses, but this number is purely theoretical, since many would probably be deemed inappropriate by the departmental head and/or dean (e.g. sociology, psychology and applied thermodynamics), and many others would be impossible to take together because of the practical problem of time-table clashes.

However, in this faculty students are required to take at least two subjects in their first year, either of which could be continued in the second and third years in single schools. The Faculty of Social Sciences offers eight single schools, twenty-four dual schools and two triple-subject schools—only thirty-four choices compared to the Arts Faculty's seventy-four.

The Arts and Social Sciences Faculties have very similar degree structures, but quite different from these two is the Faculty of Pure Science, which has a primary division between the general degree and the special degree of Bachelor of Science. In the case of the general degree, the first-year student reads three subjects from a list of eleven. After this he goes on to read two *primary* subjects for two years and one *secondary* subject for one year. There are thirteen subjects to choose from in the primary group, and for the secondary group the regulation reads:

> The secondary subject may be *either* (a) one of the
> following subjects which the candidate takes for a further
> year after passing in that subject in the First General
> Examination: Pure Mathematics, Probability and
> Statistics, Physics, Chemistry, Geology, Geography,
> Biochemistry, Psychology, *or* (b) one of the following
> subjects: Pure Mathematics, Applied Mathematics,

Computing Science, Zoology, Botany, Physiology,
Education, History and Philosophy of Science, *or* (c) one
of the following subjects at First General Examination
level, if not previously taken and if a course is provided at
suitable times and accommodation is available: Pure
Mathematics, Applied Mathematics and Computing
Science, Probability and Statistics, Physics, Chemistry,
Geology, Geography, Biology, Psychology.

Experienced academic staff are, of course, available to assist
students in choosing between the subjects in the above three
groups.

The special honours schools of the Faculty of Pure Science
are fifteen in number. Students may enter directly into these
first-year courses on the results of 'A' levels, or, with satisfactory
marks obtained in the first-year general examination, they may
transfer into the second year of a special school.

As can be seen, in this faculty the special honours schools are
less complicated than the general honours school, where it is
difficult to work out the possible combinations of individual
courses.

The Faculty of Engineering has both ordinary and honours
degrees in civil and structural engineering, control systems,
electronic and electrical engineering, mechanical engineering,
engineering with business studies, and chemical engineering and
fuel technology—six main schools of study. For the first five
of these the first-year course is partly common, and a student
can transfer from one degree course to another after first-year
courses which vary between seven and nine component parts.

The Faculty of Materials Technology has both ordinary and
honours courses leading to degrees in metallurgy, glass technology, ceramics, and materials technology—four in all. This
faculty is interesting in that it awards two differently named
degrees, a Bachelor of Metallurgy for that subject and a Bachelor
of Technical Science in the other three.

The Faculty of Law prepares almost all its students for the
ordinary or honours degree of LL.B., although a small number
of students who have read subjects other than law in their first
year transfer to this faculty to read for the degree of Bachelor
of Jurisprudence. This is done in the second and third years.
First-year LL.B. students have four set courses plus one other

course chosen from a list of twelve, only one of which is a law
subject.

The Faculty of Medicine comprises both medicine and dentistry
and these courses have very carefully prescribed regulations
which allow little choice on the part of the student. The faculty
also offers the degree of Bachelor of Medical Science which can
be taken after gaining the Second M.B., Ch.B.

The Faculty of Architectural Studies has first degrees in
architecture and in town and regional planning. A choice of
special subjects is available for third-year architects, but overall
the courses are carefully prescribed with very few options.

The most recent faculty, that of Educational Studies, has no
undergraduate students in the university, most of its work
being concerned with postgraduate degrees in librarianship and
certificates in education. It is responsible for 130 students
reading for the B.Ed. degree, but these are in colleges of
education, not the university.

The above review of the faculty structure of Sheffield University is intended to draw the reader's attention to two main
facts. The first is the complexity of the degree structures
themselves. Many people outside universities have little idea
of the complicated nature of the degree syllabuses and their
regulations, which cover 300 pages of the University Calendar
and even then are in most cases given only in outline. The
second fact of importance is the flexibility of certain degree
courses, especially in the Faculties of Arts and Social Sciences.
Generally speaking, the more vocational a degree is the less
choice the student is allowed in his syllabus. In the two main
non-vocational faculties the range of options is dazzling, and
this must have its effect upon the use of books, both in purchase
and in borrowing.

The university library

Library facilities in the university are still dominated by the
main library at Western Bank which is close to the principal
departments of the Faculties of Arts, Social Sciences, Pure
Science, Architectural Studies, Medicine and Educational
Studies. There is a major branch library at St George's Square,
where the Faculties of Engineering and Materials Technology
and the Department of Geology are provided for. The Faculty

of Law has a specialist library serviced by the main library. In addition to these libraries, however, there are numerous subsidiary libraries, some very small, which are run by academic staff at a departmental level, often at the cost of a great deal of time and effort to themselves, with very little reference to the main university library.

General data for the university library (excluding departmental libraries not under the control of the University Librarian) are in Table 3.2.[2]

Table 3.2 General data for Sheffield University Library

	1955–6	1960–1	1965–6	1970–1	1971–2
Volumes in the library at 31 July	194,708	236,460	301,993	421,318	442,671
Volumes added during the year	5,108	12,921	22,991	22,018	26,290
Discarded during the year	114	40	37	665	175
Pamphlets in the library at 31 July	21,634	24,912	35,104	47,137	50,304
Pamphlets added during the year	152	2,173	1,780	3,167	3,716
Total items in the library	221,488	276,426	361,831	492,975	522,806
Volumes borrowed by readers	33,653	61,064	76,856	106,865	118,185
Borrowed from other libraries	803	1,992	4,009	5,075	6,262
Lent to other libraries	604	1,738	2,666	3,510	3,303
Total expenditure	£12,068	£31,448	£82,957	£133,195	£157,194
% on periodicals	33	27	27	40	36
% on books	44	54	56	44	49
% on binding	21	15·5	11	10	9
% on other items	2	3·5	6	6	6
Number of volumes bound or re-bound	3,078	5,526	7,964	6,243	9,299
New subscriptions placed			373	266	308
Electrostatic copies supplied				289,521	289,721
Issues from Reserve Book Room					27,453

As Table 3.2 shows, Sheffield University library has over half a million items, over a hundred thousand borrowings a year, and an annual expenditure on books etc. (not including staff or buildings) of over £150,000. It is also interesting to note the great number of electrostatic copies supplied in the two years for which records have been published.

The great increase in the library's holdings and its general work are illustrated by the fact that between 1955–6 and 1971–2 the volumes in the library increased by over two-and-a-quarter times, and the additions in 1971–2 were more than five times as many as in 1955–6. In the academic year 1971–2 volumes borrowed were three-and-a-half times as many as in 1955–6, and the number of volumes bound (of which periodicals form a large part) was three times as many. The largest proportionate increase of all was, of course, in total expenditure, which had by 1971–2 gone up to thirteen times that of sixteen years previously. The earlier 1960s show an emphasis on expenditure on books, and then by 1970–1 there is an emphasis on periodicals. The library now subscribes to approximately 5,600 periodicals.

Whilst there is a Library Committee which meets from time to time to discuss matters of principle, the day-to-day professional running of the library is in the hands of qualified graduate staff helped by library assistants and clerical and technical staff. The purchase of items for the library is carried out under the control of the Deputy Librarian who tries to ensure that separate departments and subjects get their fair share of funds, whilst also trying to ensure that the library as a whole acquires items of general interest which may not always be asked for through the departmental network. Each department has a nominal amount of money allocated to it each year, but these funds are not inflexible and it is rare to hear of any complaints from academic staff about lack of book-funds for main-library acquisition.

Each department has a Library Correspondent whose duty it is to send forward requests for new books, periodical subscriptions and so on to the library. In some departments the professorial head may be very keen on library stocks and play a very active part in building up his subject. Others delegate the job of Correspondent to a colleague but retain a general oversight of what goes on. Yet others abdicate from, rather than delegate, the task and take little or no interest in what requests are made or how they are made. There is no overall pattern linked in any way to the type of subject; quite closely-linked departments have dissimilar interests in the library. In many cases, however, an active department does reflect a particular interest in books on the part of a professor or lecturer, and when new heads of departments are appointed there is often a new view brought to bear on library holdings, and requests increase to fill in gaps. The library is always sympathetic to book-needs for new courses, and sums of money are found to give a new course an initial boost.

Generally speaking, the interest in the library is higher in the arts than in the sciences, and in scientific and technological subjects there is often more interest shown in the acquisition of periodical literature than in books as such. It is interesting to note that, in the relatively large chemistry departmental library, periodicals are much more in evidence than are books. This does raise the question as to how much science libraries do, or should, function as information centres for data and current awareness of new developments rather than as store-houses of knowledge. Clearly the needs of students and staff in different disciplines must vary greatly and the library orders will reflect these needs.

But whilst there may be differences between the books and journals needed by different types of students, nevertheless it might be expected that all students need library facilities of some type. The current survey throws some light on what these needs are, but past studies at Sheffield give useful background material. The survey of borrowing carried out in the academic year 1960–1 by Saunders, Roberts and Wickison showed that the average borrowing per undergraduate was 11·4 items per year, made up of 10·7 books and 0·7 journals.[3] Averages for arts students were 21·0 items compared to 18·2 for social sciences including law; 8·1 for pure science; 6·8 for engineering and metallurgy taken as a group together; 4·9 for medicine; and 2·7 for dentistry. Data for the *borrowing* of journals can be misleading if certain journals are on permanent reserve or are merely referred to in the library because it is more convenient to do this than to carry a weighty bound volume about. Nevertheless, the average number of journals borrowed was, in comparative terms, outstandingly high in pure science, with

1·7 per student, whereas for the other faculties or groups figures were much lower, with engineering and metallurgy as 0·5, as was the Social Science Faculty; 0·3 for both arts and medicine; and 0·2 for dentistry. Well over half of total borrowings of journals was concentrated in one faculty, Pure Science. As a whole, 86·2 per cent of undergraduates borrowed no journals during the year, compared to 24·4 per cent who borrowed no books and 23·4 per cent who borrowed neither books nor journals.

Surveys carried out by the present writer in 1961[4] and 1965[5] for the Students' Union, to assist them in their submission to the University Grants Committee during its quinquennial visitations, found 19 per cent of students in 1961 and 17 per cent in 1965 who said that they never used any library to work in (which is not the same as borrowing from one), and this included all university libraries and public libraries. The outstanding non-use of libraries was amongst engineers (46 per cent), metallurgists (40 per cent), and medical (including dental) students (28 per cent). But whilst these proportions may seem high, it should also be borne in mind that between twenty-five and twenty-nine hours a week of formal classes were the modal category for engineers and metallurgists, and thirty to thirty-four hours for medical students. Clearly the whole form of education for such students is completely different from that of arts or social-science students with ten to fifteen hours a week in classes, with no laboratory work to do, and with reading-lists which show that staff expect a wide range of reading to be done.

Departmental libraries

Universities are complex organizations, but, unlike large business firms, they have a curiously egalitarian structure based upon the autonomy of the department—or, as some critics describe it, on the despotism of the professor. Generally speaking, the university council, senate or faculty interferes very little with the running of a department, once general principles of degree structure, staffing levels and so on have been agreed on at the appropriate higher committee levels. The body of Senate at Sheffield had eighty-six professors on it in 1971–2, along with the University Librarian, the Administrative Dean of Medicine, and eighteen representatives of the non-professorial staff. At this assembly all participants are regarded as being of equal status for the purpose of debate, but clearly the words of some carry greater weight than the words of others, and key positions on committees tend to be held by certain people. Structural problems arising from this type of 'collegial authority' are interestingly discussed by Noble and Pym,[6] although these authors do not disclose what type of organization they have based their findings on. However, outside the Senate each head of department, be it large or small, has a high degree of independence in the running of his department, and this affects the view he may hold on the provision of a departmental library.

When a special Library Development Sub-committee was set up in 1970 to consider future plans for the provision of library facilities in the university, it was necessary for the administrative staff of the Registrar's office, who were servicing the committee, to carry out an investigation to find out just how many libraries there were in the university, as the committee members were uncertain about their number and location. The resultant figure was twenty-nine departmental libraries of varied sizes and facilities in addition to the main library, the applied-science library and the physics/mathematics library. This number surprised even the committee members, who thought they knew the university fairly well, and it demonstrated very clearly how unco-ordinated departmental developments had produced a tremendous fragmentation of library resources in the university. The libraries varied greatly in seating capacity. Law had 101 seats; French, chemistry, economics/politics/business studies and one library for physiology/biochemistry (which had two departmental libraries) had seating in the 60s, but ten libraries had seating in the 20s, and six libraries seated under twenty people. These libraries were situated in a wide variety of types of room and the square footage per reader varied from 12 square feet per person in metallurgy to 55 square feet in music. Within the nineteen-storey Arts Tower, which houses the arts, social sciences and architecture departments, the square feet per reader varied from fifteen in the combined economics/politics/business studies library to forty-three in English literature.

When the Library Development Sub-committee attempted

F

to consider a plan for rationalizing the space used in the Arts Tower, so as to give fewer libraries but very little reduction in actual space available to readers, there was considerable opposition from many departments, who pointed out that these rooms were quite often the departmental 'home' for students who had nowhere else in the building to meet together (since there are no common rooms apart from one small one for architecture students on the nineteenth floor); that often the libraries were used for seminars and society meetings, for visiting speakers, even for tea-parties or evening socials; and that their loss would result in students having nowhere within the main teaching building, apart from lecture-rooms, where they could work or meet in their free hours. These very genuine appeals were in part a condemnation of a large building designed with no social facilities and an inadequate vertical transport system. Although the main university library is adjacent to the Arts Tower and linked to it by an enclosed footbridge, transport up and down the building is limited to two sixteen-person lifts (not always in working order) and a slow-moving paternoster system. Students complained that to get to and from the library for an hour between classes was too time-consuming, and that a local library for short study, using departmental books, was valuable. Nevertheless, a use-survey made by the Registrar's Department in two terms in the 1967–8 session showed that the average use being made of these libraries was less than half their actual reader capacity.

The book-stock of the semi-independent departmental libraries varies greatly. In the case of the large Chemistry Department library the intention is for most books and journals needed by students and staff to be available within the building housing chemistry. There is a departmental committee which decides on book-selection, and an unqualified assistant who is not a member of the library staff. This organization is an extreme case of a large library whose purchases are financed from the university library funds but which operates almost completely independently of it. This situation is now under review and is unlikely to continue for very much longer. On the other hand, there are smaller departmental libraries in the Arts Faculty which provide multiple copies of texts and criticisms explicitly for teaching purposes. In the case of French, for example, students are given clear reading-lists for their courses

and are told which books, especially texts, they should buy
for themselves. But there are so many critiques that students
cannot be expected to buy all of them, and so the departmental
library stocks multiple copies for reference and loan within the
department. The funds for book-purchase in most libraries of
this type come from the general departmental grant which
covers stationery, postage, departmental-staff travel expenses
and so on. Thus any money spent on books from this fund
reduces the amount available for other uses. The administration
of departmental libraries is usually carried out by, or under, an
interested member of the academic staff who may spend quite
a lot of his time on library work. In some libraries students
themselves act as library assistants, stamping books which are
borrowed and seeing that bookcases and the room are locked
in the evening when the library closes.

As can be seen from this very broad description, departmental libraries tend to specialize in teaching-books for undergraduates, and are run rather amateurishly on a somewhat
do-it-yourself basis. Control over borrowing is difficult to
exercise and the sociology department closed down its library
some years ago because of heavy losses of books and the amount
of staff time needed for stock control. Professional librarians
are generally critical of amateur-run small libraries which
operate alongside the main library but not under its control or
even in conjunction with it. Clearly a wholly rational system
of expenditure on books and journals within the university
would have more central control and co-ordination. Nevertheless, the departmental libraries are very dear to the hearts of
many academic staff and students, and socially they do
perform a valuable function in providing focal points for
departments in today's large impersonal universities. What is
needed is some form of reasonable control over monies spent
on books for all libraries and the exercising of reasonable
discretion over the amount of time that highly-paid academic
staff spend on semi-skilled aspects of library administration.

The university bookshops

The relationship between universities and bookshops is a
fascinating example of love-hate feelings. In the first place,
very few 'university' bookshops are actually *owned* by univer-

sities, though relationships may be very close indeed, as in the case of Dillon's University Bookshop in Malet Street, London, which is owned by the University of London but controlled by a board which includes non-university people and is managed by highly professional booksellers.

In the case of 'campus' universities which let university premises to booksellers (such as Nottingham, York, Essex, Canterbury, and so on) the bookshop can claim to be *the* university bookshop simply by virtue of its monopoly position on the site. But no bookshop anywhere has a genuine monopoly, since there are usually other bookshops nearby in the town (as in York, Nottingham and Canterbury), and any purchaser can obtain books by post from large bookshops such as Blackwell's, Heffer's, and the Economist Bookshop, which do a large trade in mail orders.

In the case of the 'civic' universities which have their sites not far from the town centres, it is usual to find that one or more bookshops operate in private premises on the ordinary streets close to the university site. At Sheffield the university site is now very spread out and straggling, but it is customary still to refer to the main technology departments as being at 'St George's' which is nearer to the town centre than the other departments at Western Bank, and divided from them by some old houses, a women's hospital and a church. On a main street near to St George's is Hartley Seed's bookshop, one of the two genuine 'university' bookshops in the city. Hartley Seed's began in a shop nearer the city about 1900, moved to another shop in West Street, near to St George's, in 1955 and finally moved to much larger premises, still in West Street but virtually backing on to the St George's departments, in 1967. The total shop area is 4,000 square feet and the average value of stock through the year is around £100,000 with a peak value of £150,000 at the beginning of the academic year. The public shop is mainly on the ground floor, with a smaller basement for hmso publications (for which the shop is the local agent) and children's books. The firm also has a large first floor where library supplies, schoolbooks and other 'non-shop' work are dealt with. Hartley Seed's is a general *and* university book-seller and in the one shop it offers general fiction and non-fiction, as well as educational books. Its particular strong point is technical books, and it sells regularly to students of the

Sheffield Polytechnic and colleges of further education as well as to the university. It also stocks nursing and medical books, as it is well situated near to hospitals. The shop provides stock for all university students and, whilst having a tradition of providing for the technology and medical students, it has in recent years expanded its stock to encompass law, social sciences and arts. Like all bookshops, it can, of course, order any book in print for any customer. Hartley Seed's is still a family firm, though it is now a part of the UBO (University Booksellers, Oxford) group, which is controlled by Blackwell's of Oxford.

The other university bookshop was, until recently, known as A. B. Ward's after its founder, Alan Ward, a most respected and honoured member of the British book trade. Mr Ward set up two bookshops in Sheffield—one in the centre of the town in Chapel Walk in 1927, and the other at the university, in Leavygreave in 1931. The university bookshop began in one small shop, and over the years has gradually spread into adjacent shops so that it now occupies approximately 1,200 square feet. The property is very old and scheduled for demolition by the university, which owns it, and, being a series of at least five originally separate rooms, it is far from ideal in layout. In spite of these difficulties, the present owners, Bowes and Bowes of Cambridge, have done their best to make the shop attractive with new shelving and fitments, and the result is a shop which has character and some charm. The stock is mainly university books for all subjects, though some general fiction and non-fiction is carried, mainly for student or staff leisure reading and general interests. The average stock over the year is about £30,000, with a peak value of about £50,000. Bowes and Bowes would like to have a larger shop on the same site, but discussions with the university about such developments have not yet resulted in any definite plans for a future bookshop, as the university long-term plans for this, or a similar site, have yet to be decided.

The service which these two bookshops give to the university is mainly dependent on the information given to them by the university. Since, in this context, the university means nearly 900 individual people, it is only to be expected that guidance received by the bookshops varies from excellent to non-existent. In the task of providing course-books for undergraduates, which is what we are here concerned with, the booksellers must know, as far as possible

1   What books are *expected* to be *bought* by students;
2   What books are strongly recommended, though purchase is not obligatory;
3   What books are advised reading, though purchase is not very likely.

Given these three categories, the bookseller has some order of priority for his own stocking-policy, and he may well, with a limited size of shop, decide to exclude the third category altogether.

The bookseller then needs some idea of the number of students to whom the recommendations will be made. As classes may range in size from under 5 people to over 200 students, this information is crucial. Also, if the bookseller is to have the required stock in his shop for October, when students want to buy and have just received their grants, he must have the summer in which to deal with ordering from the many publishers involved, some of whom will be overseas, and the many trade queries about new editions, books reprinting, books out of print and so on. With hundreds of titles to cope with these matters cannot be dealt with a fortnight before term begins.

In the past, the two bookshops tried to obtain information by approaching various members of staff in the departments. The method used by both shops was to send simple sheets asking for titles, authors, publishers (if known), and any special editions required. The forms also asked for the courses for which books were wanted, and the expected numbers of students. These letters went out at varying times, but usually in the summer term, earlier rather than later. Both shops varied their tactics from time to time, but generally Bowes and Bowes tried to obtain lists for a department from one known person in each department, whilst Hartley Seed's tended to send out individual letters to most members of staff. In both cases, however, there was great variation, since individual lecturers voluntarily supplied Bowes and Bowes with details, and Hartley Seed's received co-ordinated lists from certain departments.

I was kindly allowed by both bookshops to see the advice they received for the 1971–2 session, and I was able to assess the amount and type of information which they had to use to take very serious decisions about stocking what were often large numbers of expensive books. My admiration for the booksellers in the courage they showed in deciding to stock books was only matched by my conviction that the old definition of a businessman as 'a person who has to make firm decisions based on inadequate data' must have been derived from a study of university bookselling. As I was able to check some book-lists with staff in the university, it became clear that, even where the booksellers thought they were receiving good information from departments, this was often not so. The booksellers do not and cannot be expected to understand all the intricacies of the degree syllabus. Therefore, if they receive a neatly typed list, perhaps a full foolscap page long, saying that these are the key books for a first-year course in subject 'X', then the booksellers tend to think that they have done well and they are grateful to the lecturer who has supplied the information. What they frequently do not know is that the list only covers perhaps three-quarters of the needs for the course, because several of the compiling lecturer's colleagues have given him no information at all before the deadline for the list arrived. Rather obviously, the lecturer does not put at the bottom of the list that Mr A, Dr B and Professor C have failed to reply to his requests, as this would be embarrassing. When term comes, there is either a demand from students for books which Mr A has just told them about and which the bookshops have never heard of, or, as does sometimes occur, Dr B makes no recommendations at all to anyone as to which books it would be useful for students to purchase.

An interesting problem arose in October 1971 when law students descended on one bookshop asking for a first-year text not on the list which the shop had received in early summer. When the bookseller pointed out that the book recommended by Mr X on the bookseller's form was a different one from that which they were now asking for, the reply was that Mr X had changed his mind since then. The bookshop, not knowing this, had a hundred unsaleable texts in stock and no copies of the book now recommended.

Of course, lecturers themselves complain bitterly about the poor service given to them by booksellers and this is by no means restricted to Sheffield. Any group of university lecturers anywhere can always fill in the quiet half hour after lunch in trying to cap each other's stories of the ineptitude of university booksellers. The normal complaint is that, although the book-shop was told in early summer that fifty students would be recommended to buy Bloggs on *Tibetan Ceramics*, there were only three copies in the shop when term began, and subsequent orders placed by students were not delivered until after Christ-mas. The booksellers are often at fault in too timid stocking, but where there is more than one bookshop serving a university the bookshop buyer has to decide not only how many of the fifty students really *will* buy the book, but also how many will buy from his shop, how many will buy the book at home before term begins, and how many will try to get a second-hand copy. The number then actually ordered will depend greatly on the experience of past years, which can be useful but can also go wildly wrong if a lecturer changes the emphasis of his course or (even worse for the bookseller) if the lecturer leaves and is replaced by a person with different interests.

Both bookshops in Sheffield were able to supply me with numerous examples of books which, from the lecturers' lists, seemed to be absolutely essential, and yet were purchased by fewer than a quarter of the students, even taking the two bookshops' sales together. On the other hand, lecturers were able to supply me with examples of unmet demands for what they claimed were standard texts, recommended year after year. Clearly there are faults on both sides, and the bookseller can frequently pass the blame on to publishers who either do not deliver in reasonable time or else send the wrong books.

Book-selling is a curious occupation in which what might seem to be a highly rational process is frequently enlivened by extraordinary flashes of irrationality. Two examples of this may be used to show what the bookseller has to cope with.

At Hartley Seed's a young man, apparently a student, asked one of the assistants where the technology books were shelved. The assistant showed him the area of the shop where these books were on display and left him to browse. After some time the young man was asked by the assistant if he had found what he was seeking and the young man replied that he had found what he was looking for and he would now go to Bowes and Bowes to buy it.

At the Bowes and Bowes shop, near Whitsuntide, at the height of the examination season, the manager had just locked the main door at 5.30 p.m. preparatory to closing down, when a girl student knocked on the glass, seemingly in a state of some agitation. The manager reopened the door and the girl asked if he had a copy of Bennison and Wright's *The Geological History of the British Isles*, a book of some 368 pages. The manager said he thought he had one, found it and sold it to the girl. She said she was very grateful as she needed it for preparation for an examination the next morning.

Experienced booksellers learn to cope with idiosyncratic customers and can even defend themselves against irate academics, but in order to improve the two-way communications between academics and bookshops some firm structure is needed which goes beyond simply relying on the goodwill of some co-operative lecturers and despairing over the lack of interest in others.

At Sheffield there has been a Standing Committee on Bookshop Facilities since 1966, though, interestingly enough, it met in March 1971 for the first time in three years as no business had been referred to it in that period. Knowing that I was conducting research on books in the university, the Committee co-opted me. A paper on liaison between the university and bookshops was discussed, and from this a whole new scheme for bookshop liaison, devised by the Deputy Librarian (Mr Hitchens) and myself, was eventually considered and accepted by the Committee and then by Senate.[7]

The Bookshop Correspondent Scheme

The Standing Committee on Bookshop Facilities considered ways in which liaison with Hartley Seed's and Bowes and Bowes could be improved, and decided that a particular area in which improvement was needed was the system by which the bookshops were informed by the university departments about books prescribed or recommended for purchase by students for lecture courses. It was recognized that the bookshops often had to ask for this information early in the summer term, when academic staff are preoccupied with examining or preparations for examining. Requests had gone sometimes to heads of departments, sometimes to other members of staff instead or as well. The forms devised for recommendations had not always been satisfactory and the responses from departments had varied considerably: some departments had sent in comprehensive lists in good time, others had sent replies which were incomplete or late or both.

The Committee decided that this situation could be improved if a standard departmental procedure for bookshop recommendations were established and a standard form for the recommendations were designed. In doing this, the Committee took notice of an established scheme of Departmental Library Correspondents who co-ordinate the ordering of library books by their colleagues.

The scheme adopted by the Committee was that in all departments there should be a Departmental Bookshop Correspondent responsible for co-ordinating detailed information about books prescribed and recommended for purchase for courses given in the department. The information about such books would be entered on a standard form (supplied in pads) designed by the Deputy Librarian. The Departmental Correspondent would keep a carbon copy of each order and would send the top copy to the university library where it would be photo-copied, and copies would be sent to Hartley Seed's and Bowes and Bowes. The pads would have space for six books on each page, so that a departmental 'bulk order' would consist of a sheaf of pages. Each page, however, could easily be cut into six parts, which would greatly facilitate filing.

The request to the Correspondent to compile the departmental list would go out from the library early in the summer term and the Correspondent would be asked to send in his return between mid-June and mid-July. Any later additions to lists at any time during the summer or the teaching session would be made on the pads provided, and routed through the library. Once the bookshops had received their copies of recommendations from the library, direct communication between bookshops and Correspondents (or even individual lecturers) could be made to deal with problems of detail, ambiguities, delays in delivery etc.

It was suggested that the work of the Departmental Bookshop Correspondent could be conveniently done in some smaller departments by the Library Correspondent, though in larger departments it might be done by a different person. It was, however, stressed that the Bookshop Correspondent should be a lecturer of some experience and seniority, whose requests to colleagues for book recommendations could be expected to carry some weight.

The bookshops would be expected to establish personal contact with the Departmental Correspondents so as to keep them in touch with any problems in obtaining books, and they would also report to them on stocks in hand of recommended books. The standard form asks only for books which are regarded as 'essential' or 'strongly recommended' for purchase and an E or an R is placed in a box to denote this category. Correspondents are encouraged to send three copies of all reading-lists produced in the department to the library so that copies can be passed to the bookshop for information and guidance, but the new scheme attempts to make a clear distinction between books to be *bought* and books to be *read*. By concentrating on the former category it was believed that the booksellers would be spared the time and effort involved in stocking books which no one would consider buying.

The form itself is reproduced on page 201, and each sheet of the pad is made up of six forms. As can be seen, the form requires the author, title, special edition, publisher (if known), number of students, year of course and name of member of staff recommending the book. There are also the boxes 'essential' and 'recommended' for purchase of books.

The scheme was agreed by Senate early in 1972 and requests were sent out to all departments to nominate Bookshop Correspondents. In many cases, rather as expected, the current Library Correspondent took on the job, though inevitably replies from some departments took a great deal of time. The pads of forms and instructions for their use were distributed in early summer and the scheme was officially under way in the summer of 1972. General reaction was favourable and the booksellers (who make a financial contribution towards the costs) felt it had clarified the book-needs of the university. One advantage intended in the scheme was that the library will obtain information about books which previously it had never received and also that it can act as an arbiter between staff and bookshops if either group queries whether information had or had not been sent out or received.

There have still been complaints from students and staff about lack of stocks and delays in books ordered, but generally speaking it does seem that the scheme has brought about some improvement in information, and from the sociologist's point of view it is interesting to see that it linked together three groups of people who are concerned in the communication process about books.

Chapter 4

The survey of students and books

Introduction

Whilst a considerable amount of time was spent in talking to librarians, booksellers and members of the academic staff about the use of books in the university, it was felt that the only satisfactory way of obtaining facts and opinions from students was by means of a social survey. This does not mean that I did not talk informally, and even formally, to a number of students about their use of books, but, with the wide spread of subjects studied in the university and the differences between courses, the only possible way to gain any systematic rather than purely impressionistic information was to use survey methods.

To this end I decided to carry out a sample survey of all undergraduates in the university in the spring of 1972.

The sample

The survey was based on a sample of 1 in 5 (20 per cent) of all undergraduates at Sheffield University. The sample frame was the card-index of students kept by the Senior Assistant Registrar, which is the nearest thing to a 'definite' register of students in the university. The sampling was done by taking a random number between 1 and 5, which was 3, and from there on taking every fifth name from the alphabetical index of students. Wherever a postgraduate student appeared, the next card was taken, in order to obtain an undergraduate. In this way a total sample of 986 names and Sheffield addresses was obtained.

Questionnaires, along with a stamped envelope addressed to me at the Department of Sociology, were sent to all 986 people at the beginning of the seventh week of the Lent Term. This date was chosen so as to place the survey as late as possible so that students would have bought all the books needed for the session, but not so late in the term as to reduce the response through people going home in vacation. (The UGC survey noted that its response had been badly affected by being carried out late in the summer term when students were either preoccupied with examinations or had drifted away after them.)

The questionnaires addressed to students at domestic addresses were sent out through the post, and those to people in halls of residence were delivered in bulk to the appropriate porters' lodges. No questionnaires were sent to students care of their departments. The point of enclosing a *stamped* addressed envelope for reply was to enable a student to return the questionnaire via any post box. Two students did actually steam off the stamps and hand in their questionnaires to the main university porters' lodge where mail is sorted, but the rest used the GPO.

Response

Twelve letters were returned 'not-known', the bulk of which were to students who had either officially or unofficially ceased to be students but whose cards had not yet been removed from the file. The total number of completed questionnaires received was 763, giving a total response rate of 77 per cent, which for a survey of students in 1972 may be regarded as satisfactory.

As the tables show, there is a slight bias in response towards first-year students, and the distribution of respondents among the eight faculties shows a slight preponderance of pure scientists, but these are small variations and no weighting of results has been carried out.

Table 4.1   Comparative percentages of response

Year of study	Survey sample	University
First	35	33
Second	29	29
Third	31	31
Fourth or over	5	7

Faculty	Survey sample	University
Arts	17	17
Social Sciences	16	17
Architecture	4	4
Law	6	5
Medicine (incl. Dentistry)	10	12
Pure Science	30	26
Engineering	13	14
Materials Technology	4	4

The questionnaire

This is reproduced in Appendix II. It can be seen that the questions were set out on four pages, each page dealing with a separate topic. The first set of questions dealt with the guidance received by students from their lecturers about book-reading, book-borrowing and book-buying. The second page dealt with the use made by students of university library facilities. The third page dealt with the use made by students of bookshops, primarily in Sheffield. The final page asked for categorical details of the students themselves. The whole questionnaire was a carefully chosen mixture of factual and opinion questions, and each of the three main sections, whilst having pre-coded answers for several questions, deliberately ended with a completely open question where students could write in their own views and suggestions.

Analysis and results

Apart from the general results for all the 763 respondents taken together to represent all undergraduates, the principal analyses are by year of study (four categories) and by faculty (eight categories).

For simplicity of presentation and ease of reading all the results are given in percentages rounded off to the nearest whole number. In any column, therefore, the sum of the individual results will be 100 (or sometimes from 98 to 102 owing to rounding off). There seems no good reason for putting in 100 to denote the 100 per cent in every column, but a figure, denoted as n, is given for each column to show the actual *number* of replies upon which percentaging has been carried out.

This not only draws the attention of readers to columns where the overall number of cases (as in the Faculties of Law and Materials Technology) is small in itself, but also the n number can be used as a guide to non-response to certain questions. The total number of respondents overall was 763, but not every respondent answered every question, though it would be silly to exclude a whole questionnaire from analysis just because one or two questions were ignored or missed. The analysis and percentaging of replies is generally of the replies to a question, and 'no answers' are excluded from the percentaging. If, then, in the general analysis the $n =$ is well below 763, the reader is made aware of the fact that there was an appreciable non-response to this question. In a few cases where this non-response seems to be important I have commented on it.

Where sub-totals are small, as in the cases of the Faculties of Law and Materials Technology, the n for percentaging is consequently small, and it is important to recognize that a figure of, say, 13 per cent may only be four cases. Whilst the value of that percentage itself may therefore be less certain, nevertheless the percentaging of numbers, no matter how small the base, does permit comparisons to be made between years of study and between faculties.

In a number of questions the student respondents were asked to give opinions or facts on a scale, usually a five-point one. To make for even more simple comparisons between years and faculties, a scoring device has been used wherever possible. This gives a complete scale from 100 down to nil, calculated from the percentage distribution of the answers. Thus, if all respondents had ticked 'Very good' a score of 100 would have resulted. If they had all ticked 'Very poor' the score would have been 0. The actual score which results gives the reader one figure only to read and provides simpler comparisons between years and faculties than do frequency distributions.

The respondents themselves

A few details of the respondents may help 'set the scene' before the detailed analyses are given.

Sixty-nine per cent of respondents were male and 31 per cent female.

Ninety-six per cent were unmarried and 4 per cent were married.

Seventy-two per cent received more than half the standard grant from the local education authority.

Forty-eight per cent (which is disproportionately high) lived in a hall of residence, 15 per cent in lodgings, 32 per cent in flats or similar accommodation, and 1 per cent were unclassifiable.

Seventy-nine per cent were reading, or intending to read, for a single-subject degree, though many were, of course, reading additional and subsidiary courses.

The respondents were mainly in the conventional three-year degree courses and thirty-five out of thirty-eight students classified as in 'fourth-or-over' year were reading medicine or dentistry.

The next three chapters give the results of the statistical analysis, illustrated where appropriate with comments from the questionnaires and other information which helps towards explaining the problems arising.

Chapter 5

Guidance from lecturers

Introduction

As has already been shown in the theoretical model on page 5, the lecturer is in a crucial position so far as the use of books by students is concerned. Unless the lecturer informs the students about the books they should read, the students are in a position of almost complete anomie.

The first part of the questionnaire asked students about the guidance they received from their lecturers on the reading of books, about reading-lists, and about guidance on the buying of books. Finally, in this section each student was given the opportunity to offer any comments he or she wished about guidance from lecturers.

Guidance about reading

Overall, the lecturers got a fairly good rating from the students in answer to the question 'In general, do you think the guidance about reading which you receive from the lecturers on your course is: Very good; Fairly good; So-so; Poor; Very poor?' As Table 5.1 shows, nearly two-thirds of all students thought that guidance on reading was either very good (14 per cent) or fairly good (49 per cent). Only 13 per cent considered it poor (11 per cent) or very poor (2 per cent). From such a critical group as undergraduates this is surely quite a reasonable compliment to the bulk of university teaching staff.

Using the simple scoring device mentioned in chapter 4 for this question, which gives a range from 100 down to 0, the over-all rating is 66, which in academic terms might be said to give the lecturers a good upper second.

As Table 5.1 shows, the first-year students were slightly more critical than those in the second and third years. This could be partly due to the large classes in many first-year subjects, which reduce the personal contact with staff, and it can arise when a number of staff lecture on one introductory course and no one lecturer takes the responsibility for a properly co-ordinated reading-list with appropriate priorities pointed out.

Table 5.1   Lecturers' guidance (*a*)

In general, do you think the guidance about reading which you receive from the lecturers on your course is:

Very good; Fairly good; So-so; Poor; Very poor?

	All sample	1st year	2nd year	3rd year	4th year +
Very good	14	12	16	14	8
Fairly good	49	44	51	53	37
So-so	25	29	22	24	34
Poor	11	12	11	7	21
Very poor	2	3	—	2	—
$n =$	762	267	222	235	38
Score	66	63	68	68	58

'I think that the book problem is a very big one for students just starting a course and that they ought to be given more advice rather than just being presented with a book list. After all most books need to be bought in the first term.' (1st-year modern history, ancient history and English literature. £33 spent on books)

The importance of grading introductory books was made by another first-year arts student.

'A grading of the standard of the books suggested would be helpful, especially when one has never tackled a topic before.' (1st-year history, politics and geography)

This problem is put in a slightly different way by a technologist:

'The books they [lecturers] recommend are at times too technical and unreadable for the subjects they cover.' (1st-year metallurgy)

And the problem of the approach used by lecturers and authors of books is made by another technologist:

> 'Often the recommended books treat a subject in such a totally different way from the lecturer as to be virtually useless.' (1st-year civil engineering)

A student in the Faculty of Pure Science found some difficulty on a first-year course; this is common to many students:

> 'Various lecturers recommend books, but being on the Integrated Biology course it is left largely to the individual whether he buys or just reads the books. I think we could definitely do with more guidance over books for this course, especially at the start of it.' (1st-year integrated biology)

In the arts subjects the first-year students were varied in their comments. Those reading foreign languages usually had quite specific texts recommended to them, and one student commented that she had very little time for 'reading round' her subject. In English literature there were a few problems about the actual *editions* required. In history some first-year students seemed to be worried by having too many references given to them:

> 'The most common characteristic of my lecturers and tutors is that they recommend me to read and buy nearly everything.'

Though another wrote:

> 'Some lecturers swamp the student with references, others are silent on the topic. The ideal is a happy medium, and reading lists, which are sometimes provided.'

First-year students are generally regarded as being amenable to guidance in their early days, and their enthusiasm for reading must be carefully nurtured. A number of first-year students were already showing signs of disillusionment through poor guidance:

> 'It should be clearly stated where only chapters (of a book) are useful—I have wasted money over this.'
> (1st-year economics and business studies)

'Books which were said to be of great importance by Geography lecturers have been of no use whatsoever.' (1st-year geography)

'Frequently the most vague and useless History textbooks are recommended to those reading the period for the first time, instead of nice solid factual material.' (1st-year history)

Lack of thought on the part of lecturers is reflected in comments on the unavailability of recommended books:

'Mostly the advice is fairly sound but recently I have been recommended a number of books which are not available in either of the bookshops—and in the library there is only a single copy not on reserve and that is all that is available.' (1st-year economics, geography and statistics)

However, all the above comments, critical though they may be, do seem more characteristic of undergraduates than the comment from a mathematician:

'We were told that we would not need books on most courses as the notes are very good, written in full on the board.' (1st-year mathematics)

The above comments from first-year students show a wide variety of views on reading in the introductory year. Clearly the reading required for a first-year historian varies greatly from that required of a first-year materials technologist ('one book is recommended for each course') or the mathematician who claims that books are virtually unnecessary. Good guidance for beginners is of paramount importance, since first-year students at university are entering an institution which is very different from school, and ex-sixth-formers who have been accustomed to relatively small classes and perhaps very personal guidance from teachers have to adjust to a totally new environment of large classes, distant lecturers and—of overriding importance—no free books handed out to them in class.

If students become disillusioned in the first year, it will not be surprising if they become cynical in their subsequent years and if, as a consequence, buying of books declines and students come to feel that reading is not really all that necessary.

In the second and third years, students frequently find that, after the more general first-year course, the subsequent specializations within subjects lead to new problems of reading. Sometimes the references given are so numerous that the student finds he cannot keep abreast of his reading. For example:

'Lecturers recommend more books than I can ever hope to read. It is a full time job just keeping up with the lecture notes.' (3rd-year chemistry)

'We are given such good advice on cases and articles to read that if I read them all I wouldn't have time to do anything else.' (2nd-year law)

In the second and particularly third year there are problems of keeping up with all the lecture courses, writing essays or doing projects, and also trying to keep up with the recommended reading. Of course, the very long vacations which form a part of the university year (twenty-two weeks at Sheffield) are supposed to be used for reading, but no students in the survey made any comments on vacation reading.

As Table 5.1 shows, the rating on guidance for students in their fourth year or above was the lowest of all (58), but as nearly all these students were reading medicine or dentistry comment on them will be dealt with under the faculty analysis in Table 5.2.

Table 5.2 shows a relatively high degree of satisfaction about lecturers' book-guidance amongst students in the Faculties of

Table 5.2   Lecturers' guidance (*b*)

	Arts	Soc. Sci.	Arch.	Law	Med.	P.Sci.	Eng.	Mat. Tech.
Very good	29	11	17	30	6	9	4	9
Fairly good	51	68	62	54	38	44	33	53
So-so	15	13	21	13	35	34	35	25
Poor	5	6	—	2	21	11	23	9
Very poor	—	2	—	—	—	2	6	3
$n =$	129	122	29	46	78	225	101	32
Score	76	64	74	78	57	62	62	64

Arts, Architecture and Law. It is interesting to note that the highest rating is in the smallest faculty—that of Law—which is really a one-department faculty. In the Faculty of Architecture there are departments of building science and town and regional planning, as well as architecture itself, but again there is a concentration on one subject, and a type of teaching which brings students and staff into close personal contact. Also a third-year architecture student commented, 'My course does not need a lot of reading', which was confirmed to me by a lecturer adding that the students make a great deal of use of technical papers, reports and pamphlets for reference purposes.

Students in the Faculty of Arts showed much higher satisfaction than those in the remaining five faculties, and are quite distinctly more satisfied than students in the Faculty of Social Sciences, who might be considered to be reasonably similar in their reading habits to arts students, especially since several subjects are in both faculties.

It would seem that in the languages departments of the Arts Faculty, where set books, texts and critiques loom large in the curriculum, the general guidance about reading satisfies most students. Some departments even receive unsolicited compliments from students:

'I feel our department is excellent in this respect. One lecturer even asks if *we* have any books to recommend, which is helpful.' (2nd-year English language and literature)

'Guidance is always helpful and practical.' (3rd-year biblical studies)

But where courses of study do not have what could be called 'set books' at the centre of the syllabus, the guidance seems less satisfactory and students receive either a plethora of advice or too little:

'Often no priority is given to certain books which are perhaps essential. As a result one wastes time reading unimportant books.' (2nd-year history and politics)

'Some lecturers are very vague as to what books to buy or read at all. And sometimes books are suggested to be bought and they are not useful after a very short time.' (1st-year German, geography and sociology)

One second-year student of philosophy and politics summed up his feelings as follows:

'It is not that guidance is bad, but one has to be pushy to get worthwhile guidance from lecturers. One feels reticent to go to lecturers for advice over books partly because of personal diffidence, partly through their blasé and rather patriarchal attitude.'

The unco-ordinated nature of guidance is made evident by two social scientists. One, a third-year psychologist, wrote:

'From the lecturers that bother, the guidance is very helpful.'

Whilst a third-year sociologist wrote:

'Generally, if I ask for information of this type it is given.'

In both these cases the students seem to be damning with faint praise.

In the Faculty of Pure Science comments were varied and even contradictory. One second-year zoologist wanted 'a wider range of recommended books from which students could select their own choices', while a third-year zoologist complained of 'so many books being advised that time is only available to read a small fraction of them.'

More generally, however, a second-year physics student commented:

'The lecturers seem to prefer the student who learns his notes and then reads, reading being secondary. More encouragement to read is necessary in the Pure Science Faculty.'

Also a third-year geologist made the comment:

'Many of the books we have been recommended are out of print. This seems to be a fairly common occurrence in science courses.'

However, students reading chemistry, mathematics, microbiology, genetics and biochemistry had complimentary comments to offer, some of them pointing out that in the smaller departments there was 'close contact with the staff and it is easy to ask their advice'.

This approachability of lecturers was echoed by a third-year mechanical engineer:

'I have found that whenever I require reading material the lecturers have been very approachable and advice freely given.'

This particular quotation is very interesting and well justifies closer analysis. This student goes to the lecturers when he *requires* reading-material, which is a very different picture from the historian or social scientist who seems almost submerged under his lengthy reading-lists. Perhaps this indicates an important difference in the usage of books between different subjects. We have already met the mathematician who claimed that no books were necessary and the physicist who felt that reading came second-best to lecture notes. This indicated that, from these students' viewpoint, reading is a supplementary or ancillary activity to buttress the lectures and practical work, but not at the core of the learning process. To apply this sort of viewpoint to a course in, say, history, politics or sociology would be inconceivable: indeed, some social scientists seem to eschew even textbooks simply because they *are* textbooks and not 'original' in their thinking. The engineering approach based on one textbook was noted by a student who commented that:

'Some lecturers mention only one textbook, often one written by themselves, others seldom mention books at all.'

In general, then, in courses which are factual and technical and less based upon opinions and subjective viewpoints, the teaching can make more use of textbooks—or even be based primarily on lectures, explanations, practical examples and laboratory work. This way of teaching may be said to typify the 'doing' subjects rather than the 'talking' subjects. There are particular problems of guidance in the Faculty of Medicine, where students of medicine and dentistry are involved in learning practical skills based upon scientific knowledge. Medical students were the most critical of all about guidance in reading, and comments came especially from those in the clinical stages of their training. The problem is basically that the medical syllabus (i.e. medicine, not dentistry) is a very heavy one which requires students to learn the basic steps in a wide range of specialisms from teachers who are usually of consultant status in their own special fields. The gap between teacher and taught is a wide one and so, as one sixth-year medical wrote,

> 'Consultants expect students to know too much about their own specialities and invariably suggest large unreadable books on their own subjects. Students would benefit from smaller works for routine reading even if they are not as good or as comprehensive. A readable book won't spend all its life gathering dust on a bookshelf.'

This type of comment was also made by fourth-year students, one of whom wrote, 'Most lecturers assume you will use large textbooks when in fact most students use the shortest ones possible and few lecturers tell us about these.'

This use of smaller, un-recommended books by medical students was verified to me by an ex-medical bookseller in another city, who told me that at his shop he had a special selection of the shorter and cheaper books for each year of the medical course and when students came in with their official reading-lists, bewailing the cost of the large volumes recommended, the bookseller was able to offer them an alternative 'package' at much smaller bulk and lower price. Objective evidence gave no indication of this having any effect on the failure rate at the medical school.

To sum up on this section, it would appear from the statistical tables and the free comments of the students that, although the overall guidance from lecturers is generally good rather than bad, nevertheless there is a lot of room for improvement in many subjects. But books are not used in a uniform way in all the various faculties and departments of the university, and it is important, at this stage of the analysis, to appreciate that guidance on the use of books by lecturers must be made appropriate to the subject being taught, and what might be an appropriate form of reading for an arts or social science subject would be quite wrong for a technological or medical one.

Lecture courses and reading-guidance

When a student is said to be reading for a degree in, say, German or chemical engineering, he is in fact probably taking anything between three and a dozen different specialist courses which will eventually form the basis for his final examinations.

At Sheffield all students in the first-year courses in the Faculties of Arts and Social Sciences take three different *subjects*, and in their second and third years, even in single-honours schools, they will probably take between eight and ten separate *courses* within the one subject.

Although it is very difficult to say what *exactly* is a lecture course it was felt that it would be worth asking undergraduates how many lecture courses they were taking, so as to assess the broad differences between years and faculties. The results are given in Tables 5.3 and 5.4.

Table 5.3 Lecture courses (a)

How many lecture courses are you taking this year?			... courses

No. of courses	All sample	1st year	2nd year	3rd year
3 or less	24	40	15	12
4 or 5	23	19	23	26
6 or 7	19	12	22	23
8 or 9	13	12	16	12
10 or more	21	17	23	25
$n =$	734	261	214	228

As Table 5.3 shows, 40 per cent of first-year students are attending three or fewer lecture courses, which reflects the three-subject first-year courses in the Faculties of Arts and Social Sciences and some sections of Pure Science. In the second and third years students take more courses. The 'fourth-year-and-more' category, being so heavily weighted by medical students, has been omitted from this table.

The faculty analysis shows some interesting differences between types of subjects. For example 87 per cent of the Law Faculty students say they have only four or five lecture courses, whereas in Materials Technology 94 per cent have ten courses or more, with a figure of 61 per cent at this level in the Engineering Faculty. Students who have a large number of actual lecture courses may find that this fragmentation of teaching leads more to the use of selected textbooks and makes reading round a

Table 5.4 Lecture courses (*b*)

No. of courses	Arts	Soc. Sci.	Arch.	Law	Med.	P.Sci.	Eng.	Mat. Tech.
3 or less	45	25	4	9	37	26	4	3
4 or 5	14	32	30	87	34	16	3	—
6 or 7	22	26	18	4	8	27	8	—
8 or 9	11	16	33	—	12	11	24	—
10 or more	8	2	15	—	9	21	61	94
n =	123	121	27	46	68	222	96	31

course more difficult. Students were asked if there were any lecture courses for which they thought the guidance about reading was inadequate and, as Tables 5.5 and 5.6 show, nearly two-thirds of all students had at least one lecture course in which reading-guidance was inadequate.

Table 5.5 Lecture courses and guidance (*a*)

Are there any courses for which you think the guidance about reading is inadequate?

Yes; No   If Yes, how many courses?   . . . courses

No. of courses	All sample	1st year	2nd year	3rd year	4th year +
No	37	38	39	33	34
Yes, 1	21	22	20	22	9
Yes, 2	16	14	15	18	16
Yes, 3	10	12	5	12	13
Yes, 4 or 5	9	6	11	9	12
Yes, 6 or 7	5	5	6	4	13
Yes, 8 or 9	1	1	1	1	3
Yes, 10 or more	2	2	1	3	—
n =	729	257	214	226	32

As Table 5.5 indicates, inadequacy of guidance is fairly evenly distributed through the first three years of study, though in the third year there is an increase in dissatisfaction. The fourth-year-and-over group, being dominated by medical students, is best viewed by referring to Table 5.6 for faculty analysis.

Table 5.6   Lecture courses and guidance (*b*)

No. of courses	Arts	Soc. Sci.	Arch.	Law	Med.	P.Sci.	Eng.	Mat. Tech.
No	53	33	54	58	42	30	24	16
Yes, 1	25	37	21	24	15	20	5	6
Yes, 2	13	20	11	13	16	18	11	13
Yes, 3	4	6	11	2	16	12	16	13
Yes, 4 or 5	2	4	4	2	4	12	17	29
Yes, 6 or 7	2	1	—	—	4	6	13	15
Yes, 8 or 9	—	—	—	—	1	—	5	3
Yes, 10 or more	—	—	—	—	—	2	7	6
$n =$	126	120	28	45	67	215	96	32

Table 5.6 is affected by the numbers of courses shown in Table 5.4, and so the large proportions of students in the Faculties of Engineering and Materials Technology who have inadequate reading-guidance in four or more lecture courses are reflecting a proportionate figure allied to the large number of courses they take, compared with, say, law or arts students. Only in the Faculties of Arts, Architecture and Law do a majority of students say that they have *no* lecture courses in which their reading-guidance is inadequate. In Medicine the position is better than average; the Social Sciences and Pure Science are just below average; and in Engineering and Materials Technology the position is well below average.

Comments on lecture courses and general guidance illustrated a number of problems faced by students. A third-year law student commented that there was 'some conflict between two lecturers in one course. They recommend different standard textbooks.' A third-year student of town and regional planning noted that they did not always receive book-lists for their assignments. A third-year history student commented, 'Whether or not there is adequate guidance depends very much on individual lecturers. Lecturers have been known not to give any at all, even on request, until pressed by the head of department after complaints [from students].'

Lack of co-ordination of reading by students frequently stems from degree courses with a large number of lecture courses and an apparent lack of communication between lecturers about prescribed reading:

'Many of my courses overlap and therefore so do the books. It would save time and money if lecturers used a common book where possible.' (1st-year electrical engineering)

A further reference to the self-centred attitude of lecturers giving individual courses comes from a second-year geography student who claimed to have spent £60 on books during the year:

'If lecturers would only remember that their course is not the only one we happen to be studying and would point out essential books, preferably the paperback editions.'

The connection between the lecturers and the references used in preparation by the lecturers themselves was made by two students:

'They [lecturers] should say which book is their own main reference source for the lectures.' (1st-year architecture)

'Some lecturers take their notes from and give references to books that are not in the library, not in the Reserve Book Room and are too expensive to buy.' (2nd-year statistics)

Printed or duplicated reading-lists

Since dictating reading-lists to students is a tedious business and names and titles often require spelling out, many lecturers produce printed (or duplicated) reading-lists for their students. Such lists can be issued in October for the whole of the forth-coming session, or at intervals during a course as new sections of the course begin. In some departments, or even faculties, complete reading-lists for the year are issued to all students. However, not all staff favour committing themselves to paper in advance of a course of lectures which they may well change whilst it is being given. Other lecturers undoubtedly find the work of preparing a reading-list too much for them.

The whole question of formal reading-lists is an important aspect of reading-guidance and so students were asked some questions about this. The first question was a fairly general one with a categorical rather than numerical answer. The results of it are given in Tables 5.7 and 5.8. Somewhat to my own personal surprise less than half the undergraduates claimed to receive printed lists for 'all' or 'most' of their lecture courses.

Table 5.7   Reading-lists (a)

In general do you receive printed (duplicated) reading-lists for the courses you take?

All; Most; Some; Few; None

	All sample	1st year	2nd year	3rd year	4th year +
All	13	13	14	12	11
Most	28	27	28	33	11
Some	18	15	19	19	18
Few	25	24	21	26	39
None	16	21	17	10	21
$n =$	762	267	222	235	38
Score	49	49	50	53	38

As Table 5.7 shows, 41 per cent of all students say that they receive printed (or duplicated) reading-lists for only 'few' or even 'none' of their courses, and the figure is 45 per cent in the crucial first year. As usual, the people at fourth year or more are affected strongly by the medical students at the clinical stage and here the 'few' or 'none' figure is 60 per cent.

Between the various faculties, law students are outstandingly the best-supplied, with 80 per cent receiving printed lists in all or most of their courses. Arts, Social Sciences and Architecture Faculties do reasonably well, with about two-thirds in

Table 5.8   Reading-lists (*b*)

	Arts	Soc. Sci.	Arch.	Law	Med.	P.Sci.	Eng.	Mat. Tech.
All	27	13	10	29	15	4	3	22
Most	40	51	55	51	14	20	2	13
Some	19	31	24	9	18	17	6	6
Few	11	4	10	7	38	37	35	41
None	2	1	—	4	14	21	54	19
n =	129	122	29	45	78	226	101	32
Score	69	68	66	69	44	37	16	45

these two categories. Materials Technology, Medicine and Pure
Science show a general decline, beginning at below half, and in
Engineering 89 per cent of students claim to receive reading-
lists in few or none of their courses. Generally speaking, the
humanities-sciences division is shown quite strongly in this
table. A first-year metallurgy student explained, 'Books are

Table 5.9   Numbers of reading-lists (*a*)

Are there any courses for which you do not receive any printed (duplicated) reading-lists?

Yes; No   If Yes, how many courses?   ... courses

No. of courses	All sample	1st year	2nd year	3rd year	4th year +
No	23	26	22	19	31
Yes, 1	21	24	15	23	17
Yes, 2	14	11	15	17	7
Yes, 3	9	7	11	9	10
Yes, 4 or 5	12	12	13	9	17
Yes, 6 or 7	8	6	11	7	7
Yes, 8 or 9	4	4	4	3	—
Yes, 10 or more	10	10	9	13	10
n =	726	261	209	227	29

suggested for reading and buying but very few duplicated lists are supplied.' This statement is rather surprising, since the Faculty of Materials Technology publishes a concise list each year, recommending basic textbooks for purchase.

A more quantitative question put to the student respondents asked them to say if there were any lecture courses for which they did not receive printed reading-lists, and if so how many? Tables 5.9 and 5.10 show that about three-quarters of all students had at least one such course, and many had more.

Table 5.9 reinforces the picture given in Table 5.7 of higher incidence of lack of reading-lists in the first year and the fourth and further years.

Table 5.10 Numbers of reading-lists (*b*)

No. of courses	Arts	Soc. Sci.	Arch.	Law	Med.	P.Sci.	Eng.	Mat. Tech.
No	40	34	15	37	30	10	6	30
Yes, 1	29	30	33	46	23	13	6	—
Yes, 2	16	16	19	7	15	19	3	—
Yes, 3	6	11	15	4	14	12	3	7
Yes, 4 or 5	8	6	14	7	8	21	7	—
Yes, 6 or 7	2	3	4	—	6	15	13	7
Yes, 8 or 9	—	1	—	—	2	1	17	10
Yes, 10 or more	—	—	—	—	3	8	44	43
n =	125	122	27	46	66	215	95	30

Table 5.10 reflects the general humanities-sciences division shown in Table 5.8, and shows that, at best, as in the Faculty of Arts, at least 60 per cent of students have at least one course of lectures for which they do not receive a printed reading-list. Some of the comments from students help to explain whether or not the absence of printed reading-lists is of great importance to them. One arts student clearly does not find this a deprivation:

'By their very nature most of the courses, e.g. translation, introductory courses to new languages, conversation hours etc., do not require long printed reading lists and

H

the lecturer will, if necessary, read out a book reference before the lecture.' (2nd-year German)

A first-year student in the Pure Science Faculty reacts differently:

'There are very few recommended texts for mathematics students and I think it would be a good idea to issue at the beginning of each term a list of all books recommended for our course rather than be told in lectures by each individual teacher.' (1st-year applied mathematics)

From the Engineering Faculty, a student's comment reflects the problems of fragmentation of teaching:

'When dealing with individual topics in a course no list is given of books or sections in books dealing with that topic. This would be helpful since, if there was any difficulty with a certain subject, reference could be made to the appropriate books.' (3rd-year electrical engineering)

And an interesting comment from another technologist:

'Our course is applied science and I do not think much reading is necessary so apparently the lecturers do not give us any lists. Their advice on book buying is good, but if I bought all the books recommended I would have a library of my own.' (1st-year materials technology)

In all fairness to this materials technologist, he had spent £31 already on books, so he was some way towards having a library of his own even if, at this stage, he was still unconvinced of its desirability.

Of course it cannot be assumed that simply because a lecturer *does* provide a printed reading-list the list is a good one. Perhaps any list is better than none at all (though even this seems debatable) but a bad list could certainly mislead, confuse and irritate the recipients. Those people who had received printed reading-lists were therefore asked to say what they thought of them, and Tables 5.11 and 5.12 analyse their views.

Table 5.11 indicates a general satisfaction about the reading-lists with not very much variation between the first three years. For the most part only about 10 per cent of students consider

Table 5.11 Quality of reading-lists (*a*)

In general do you think the reading-lists you do receive are:
Very good; Good; So-so; Poor; Very poor?

	All sample	1st year	2nd year	3rd year	4th year +
Very good	10	9	13	11	3
Good	48	50	47	51	27
So-so	31	30	32	30	48
Poor	7	7	5	6	15
Very poor	3	3	3	2	6
n =	686	228	206	219	33
Score	63	63	66	66	51

the lists 'poor' or 'very poor', though it would be better if more of the 31 per cent giving only a 'so-so' rating had given a 'good'. Overall, however, there seems to be a reasonably satisfied reaction from students about those lists that are circulated, and certainly many of the lists that I collected from various departments and faculties during the research showed that careful thought had been given to helping students in their studies. Only a minority would, in my opinion, confuse and exasperate the recipient.

Table 5.12 Quality of reading-lists (*b*)

	Arts	Soc. Sci.	Arch.	Law	Med.	P.Sci.	Eng.	Mat. Tech.
Very good	15	11	14	23	3	9	9	—
Good	66	54	48	57	30	43	29	59
So-so	17	30	31	11	42	40	40	28
Poor	1	5	7	7	19	7	10	7
Very poor	1	1	—	2	6	2	12	7
n =	127	121	29	44	69	199	68	29
Score	73	68	67	73	51	63	53	60

As Table 5.12 shows, the medicals and engineers were the most critical of the reading-lists they *did* receive and in both these faculties students had remarked on a lack of reading-lists in the first place. The Law Faculty and the Arts Faculty came out well, and Social Sciences and Architecture lead Pure Science and Materials Technology. The problems of compiling good reading-lists can be very great if the lecturer is striving to hit a good balance between not leaving out essential references and yet not burdening the students with an over-abundance of books and articles. That there are real problems was shown by the large number of comments made by students on this point. We begin with an extreme case:

> 'Enclosed is a book list for a course already covered this year. It was accompanied by comment that all the books should be read.' (The list contained 67 books. PHM)
> (1st-year architecture)

Another first-year architect commented that 'It would help if lecturers made sure that books on the reading list are not out of print. One has been for 12 years.'

This worry about books being unavailable was reiterated by a third-year philosophy student. 'No consideration is given to the availability of books. Some aren't even in the libraries and even turn out to be out of print—even set course books.'

Many arts students were clearly worried by the length of reading-lists given to them:

> 'It is often the case that a list will not tell you which are the important books. You can waste time reading only slightly connected books.' (3rd-year English and philosophy)

On foreign-languages courses there are problems from the students' viewpoint:

> 'The lecturers tend to give exhaustive lists of criticisms and editions of books. Many of the books recommended have too tenuous links with the course and are therefore a waste of time on a heavy course when one could have been reading something more profitable.' (1st-year arts, reading French and German)

Reading-lists *plus* guidance from lecturers are obviously the ideal combination so far as some students are concerned:

'Obviously standard text listing is useful; so would be
more individual advising from lecturers/tutors. Chatty
comment-laden booklists are better than a cold series
of titles.' (2nd-year English and politics)

A third-year French student had obviously given careful
thought to the following comment:

'I have nearly always found the reading lists themselves
perfectly adequate but I would have appreciated some
indication as to how many books on these lists can
feasibly be read. In the 2½ years I have been at university
I have never known if I am reading enough or too many
books on a particular course.'

If this is a difficulty for a student reading for a single-subject
degree, how much more of a problem it is for the student who
has chosen to read for a triple-subject degree:

'Some of my lecture groups consist of a hotch-potch of
single honours, dual honours and combined subjects
[i.e. triple honours PHM], consequently some individuals
are required to extract [sic] greater or lesser knowledge.
In this case it would help the non-specialist if there was a
skeleton reading list incorporated in the more comprehensive list written for single honours students.' (3rd-year
arts, combined subjects)

Overlong book-lists for particular lecture courses were commented on by some social scientists:

'Although most reading lists are good and have some
bearing, some lecturers tend to give book lists which are
too long and unrealistic. For example, for one course
I have received a book list of over 100 references for a
course of 30 lectures. Such a number is ridiculous when
one considers this course is one fifth of my full course
this year. Perhaps the person concerned considers reading
500 books in a year is not excessive.' (2nd-year politics)

A first-year student reading economics, accountancy and law
wrote, 'I feel most students are so put off by the length of
reading lists that they tend to give up and neglect essentials
along with fringe reading.' And another first-year social
scientist reading economics, sociology and psychology felt that

'Lecturers suggest too many introductory books at the beginning of the year. Then first-year keenness causes waste of money and disenchantment with the validity of booklists.'

The lack of relevance of some books listed is commented on by a second-year psychology student and a third-year dentistry student. The psychologist comments that 'The booklist at the beginning of the year for basic texts on each of the courses generally includes books never referred to again during the year as essential', whilst the dentist gives practical advice, 'Ignore printed book lists and concentrate on the books mentioned by the lecturer. The same book list has probably been in use from the turn of the century.'

In the Faculty of Pure Science there seem to be some differences between the biological sciences and other subjects. In human biology a second-year student suggests, 'Lecturers should be more specific on set books instead of giving large numbers of alternatives.' And in the first-year integrated biology course a student writes, 'It would help if we were told the relevant chapters of books on the reading list and how much detail to read into these.' By contrast, a third-year pure mathematics student asks for 'More printed lists covering not just the main books but also ones with slight references to the course.'

Two third-year pure science students offer comments which help the outsider to understand better how they themselves see their own subjects and their learning processes:

'In Pure Mathematics the notes are more or less
self-contained. A list of books, basically for reference,
is given by most, if not all, lecturers. For Statistics,
however, books treating the subject in a similar way to
the course can be hard to come by.' (3rd-year pure
mathematics and statistics)

'We are not given reading lists as such but a number of
references to chemical journals in each lecture. These are
not all meant to be read but are helpful in the event of
not understanding a section of the work. Lecturers do
not recommend books to *buy* as perhaps only one or
two chapters would be relevant.' (3rd-year chemistry)

This *not* recommending books to be bought is repeated by a technology student:

'Most of the books recommended are not meant to be
bought.' [But then comes the sting] 'They are also often
not in the libraries.' (3rd-year chemical engineering)

And a first-year student of materials technology also affirms
that 'Some of the books recommended for reading, although
necessary are unavailable in the University libraries.'

So there are differences in the guidance which students
expect from their lecturers, according to the type of subject
they are studying. For many arts and social science students
there seem to be too many books being advised and listed
without differentiation or priority. But some scientists and
technologists who do not feel the need for many books express
disappointment that even the limited numbers of titles referred
to are by no means always available to them in library or
bookshop.

Guidance from lecturers on book-buying

Britain differs from many other European countries in that
virtually all books needed by young people in *schools* are
provided free of charge by the local education authority. There
is no tradition at all in this country of schoolchildren, even in
the sixth form, being expected to buy their own books. Obviously many young people of reasonable literacy do become
book-buyers at quite an early age, but it has previously been
noted that in this era of expansion many young people entering
higher education come from homes where there are not many
books about.

When these young people begin at university they have a
maintenance grant, which contains a nominal amount of money
for books, equipment and materials. For the session 1971-2
this was £48, for 1972-3 it was £51, and for 1973-4, £54. This
can be quite a large sum of money to be spent for young people
who have perhaps never normally bought anything more than
a cheap paperback and who may now be expected to purchase
a basic textbook costing near, or even over, £10. Guidance on
buying is therefore not only an important part of the lecturers'
educational function; it also contributes to an important form
of social and financial training.

An eminent and highly sympathetic university bookseller

has commented to me on the timidity shown by many new university students when they come to his shop to buy their first books. Some are even accompanied by their parents. Some come in clutching sheets of reading-lists and buy any title they can find on these lists—important or peripheral. I have myself noticed how some new students walk about with a textbook in hand or under the arm, as if the knowledge in it will eventually leave the book and enter them by some form of diffusion. For the new student, books are indicators of *being* at the university. Guidance on *how* to buy the right ones must originate from the lecturers.

All the respondents in the survey were asked whether they did receive guidance from their lecturers on what books to buy. The results are in Tables 5.13 and 5.14.

Table 5.13   Guidance on book-buying (*a*)

Do you receive guidance from your lecturers about what books to *buy*?
All; Most; Some; Few; None

	All sample	1st year	2nd year	3rd year	4th year +
All	18	21	17	17	21
Most	35	37	38	31	37
Some	27	27	29	27	29
Few	16	13	14	21	11
None	3	2	3	6	3
$n =$	761	266	221	236	38
Score	62	66	64	59	66

As Table 5.13 shows, only 53 per cent of all students claim that they receive guidance on book-buying from 'all' or 'most' of their lecturers. Nearly one in five says he gets such guidance from a 'few' or even 'none' of his lecturers. Guidance declines from the first year through the second to the low point of the third year. Students in the fourth year or more (mainly medicals) are almost identical with first-years. Though it may be heartening that the new, first-year students report the most guidance, a rating of sixty-six with 42 per cent of students gaining advice from no more than 'some' lecturers, does not seem a startlingly good send-off to university book-buying.

Analysis by faculties gives some interesting differences.

Table 5.14   Guidance on book-buying (*b*)

	Arts	Soc. Sci.	Arch.	Law	Med.	P.Sci.	Eng.	Mat. Tech.
All	14	7	10	57	22	15	23	25
Most	18	24	34	33	44	44	43	47
Some	29	35	52	7	24	25	26	28
Few	27	31	3	4	10	13	7	—
None	12	3	—	—	—	3	—	—
$n =$	127	122	29	46	78	226	101	32
Score	49	50	62	86	70	64	70	74

The Law Faculty (with a score of eighty-six) comes out well ahead of the others on guidance on book-buying and, interestingly, is followed by Materials Technology with seventy-four. Medicine and Engineering tie for third place with seventy, and Pure Science comes in fifth with sixty-four. Architecture is sixth with sixty-two, Social Sciences seventh with fifty, and Arts least with forty-nine. This order again draws our attention to two important factors. First there is the homogeneity of the small faculty—well exemplified by Law and to a lesser degree by Materials Technology, and second there is the broader arts-sciences division. We have already learned how some Arts Faculty book-lists tend to be long and undifferentiated, so it is not surprising to find that in such cases the students get little help in what to buy for themselves. Put simply—if the lecturer is not specific about what he wants a student to *read*, he is even less likely to be specific about what to *buy*.

Two students in the Faculty of Arts differentiated between books for reading and books for buying:

> 'As I do an English course most of the books I buy are set texts and we are recommended to buy very little other than these.' (3rd-year English)

'Reading guidance is usually for specialised topics; book buying guidance is usually for general works of reference and introductory works.' (3rd-year pre-history and archaeology and ancient history dual)

But a second-year student of history and politics complains that 'More guidance is needed on the type of books one should buy. On some courses no books are recommended for buying at all.'

In the social sciences there seems to be an important consideration of the costs of books. A third-year psychologist wrote, 'One cannot possibly afford all the books they [the lecturers] say you should buy'—though he had only spent £15 himself that year.

A third-year geography student was clearly annoyed that 'Too many lecturers recommend their own books—most of which are above average cost and have only one necessary section in them. Students feel obligated [*sic*] to buy these as they are "worried" that there will probably be an examination question on this particular topic.'

A first-year student of sociology, economics and accountancy, writing at the end of the Lent Term, had clearly already learned economic caution when he wrote, 'I am afraid I have not bought any books yet.' By contrast, a third-year economist, who wrote 'We don't need to buy too many books since most of the information comes from periodicals', had nevertheless spent between £15 and £20.

Although law students were the most satisfied of all with their lecturers' guidance on book-buying, one second-year student did comment, 'Lecturers tend to tell you to buy books regardless of their value to the course. In fact less books are necessary than they suggest.' And a first-year lawyer felt that 'Many first years would appreciate a best-buy guide before they come up to the university. Only the cool headed ones dare wait more than a few days before buying. Suggestions in lectures often come too late, so that optimum book buying is not accomplished.'

In the Faculty of Medicine one first M.B. student simply wrote that 'Book buying advice could not be improved on.' But a second-year student felt there was 'A lack of advice on whether or not purchase of particular books is worthwhile. But guidance on books is usually attained [*sic*] from students of previous years'—and he had spent £38 so far that year.

A third-year dentistry student said that 'Most lecturers do not commit themselves on buying books. They issue a list and leave the choice to the students. I prefer lecturers to be specific in advising which books to buy.'

In the Faculty of Pure Science a first-year student on the integrated biology course did not seem to expect to be able to obtain books needed from the local bookshops:

'Hardly any guidance whatsoever has been given as regards book reading. The main comment I can make about book buying is that we are advised too late. By the time we start ordering it is so late that it is half way through the term when we get the books from the bookshops. Booklists should be sent out well in advance of the start of each session or term.'

Some first-year chemistry students felt that they needed better guidance on buying, as some of them had bought books right at the beginning of the year which turned out not to be worth purchasing. By contrast, a second-year student of genetics and microbiology wrote, 'Most lecturers say it is not worth actually buying the books, and to get them out of the library.' A first-year mathematics student went even further and said, 'We are not required to buy any books as the lecture notes are very comprehensive'. Actually, he did claim to have spent £5.60 during the year.

In the Faculty of Engineering there was clearly a great deal of attention paid to the availability of books in the library as an alternative to purchase:

'We are generally asked not to buy any books but to use them as references at the well-stocked library. I agree with this policy due to the prohibitive cost of books.' (3rd-year electrical engineering)

But another technologist commented:

'The cost of books is high and most books recommended for purchase are about £3 or over. Other books recommended for reference cannot be found in department libraries or other libraries.' (3rd-year chemical engineering)

And in materials technology a second-year student wrote,
'Lecturers should realise that their lecture course is only a small part of a year's work and so it is stupid to recommend a £5 book to buy.'

This student had spent £20 himself.

When students with a nominal amount of £48 for books, stationery and equipment feel that books priced at £3 are over-expensive, then clearly they must have a very special viewpoint on technical books in the present day. The general tenor of the remarks from medicals, scientists and technologists indicated an attitude to the books which they had to have as being expensive—though strangely enough the law students made few complaints about their costly books. From these comments a hypothesis may be derived that when students have to work *from* specific books, as with language texts, law books and some science books, they recognize the central function of books in their education. But when books are a matter of choice (as in the more descriptive social sciences) or are for reference almost apart from the taught course (as in mathematics or some technologies), then the student quickly questions the *necessity* of having books in his actual possession. So this really adds up to the point that, for a student to accept the *necessity* of buying books for himself, he must be in a position where he could not do the course at all without them—they must be the actual tools of the job. And so the attitude of the mathematician with no books is probably quite rational: he genuinely does not feel that his course of study requires him to use them. What is more surprising is that there are students of the social sciences who feel the same way.

Monetary considerations *are* important to students with a total grant of £445 in 1971–2, living away from home for thirty weeks of the year. It was interesting to see that some students did not begrudge spending money on books, but they were annoyed when their scarce resources were wasted because of poor guidance from their lecturers.

> 'I have tended to buy those books which appear in the Faculty Handbook as set texts, only to be told by a lecturer that another edition is better. Consistency would be helpful.' (2nd-year English, and £35 spent)

'When recommending books lecturers should say whether
they are merely useful to read or whether it is imperative
to buy them. To begin with I bought when I merely
had to read a dozen pages.' (3rd-year philosophy, and
£27 spent)

Such questioning of guidance can quickly lead to cynicism.

'I wonder if lecturers read the books they recommend.
In one or two instances the books recommended have been
next to useless.' (1st-year economics, accountancy and
geography)

To evaluate the quality of lecturers' guidance on book buying,
the students were asked a direct question on this topic, and
Tables 5.15 and 5.16 give the answers.

Table 5.15   Quality of buying-guidance (*a*)

Do you consider the guidance on what books to *buy* is:

Very good; Good; So-so; Poor; Very poor?

	All sample	1st year	2nd year	3rd year	4th year +
Very good	6	5	8	8	3
Good	45	46	44	43	61
So-so	33	34	34	33	21
Poor	12	13	11	11	11
Very poor	4	2	4	5	5
n =	754	265	220	231	38
Score	59	60	61	60	62

As Table 5.15 shows, the general score is fifty-nine and there
are only slight fluctuations between the years. Overall, 51 per
cent of students give a rating of 'good' or 'very good', but this
means that virtually half gave no better than a 'so-so'. Also the
rating of fifty-nine is lower than the score of sixty-six for
general guidance on reading and sixty-three for the quality of
the reading-lists issued.

Table 5.16   Quality of buying-guidance (a)

	Arts	Soc. Sci.	Arch.	Law	Med.	P.Sci.	Eng.	Mat. Tech.
Very good	8	3	7	30	4	4	5	3
Good	35	32	52	50	50	48	52	72
So-so	29	41	31	11	33	35	37	25
Poor	19	17	10	7	12	11	5	—
Very poor	9	6	—	2	1	3	1	—
$n =$	125	121	29	46	78	225	98	32
Score	54	52	64	75	61	60	64	70

As Table 5.16 giving analysis by faculties demonstrates, satisfaction on buying-guidance was, not unexpectedly, highest in the Faculty of Law, followed by Materials Technology; Engineering and Architecture tied for third place; then came Medicine, Pure Science, Arts; and last of all the Social Sciences.

In the Faculty of Arts some students commented on the amounts of money which could be involved if they bought everything recommended to them. The most satisfied arts and social sciences students were those who felt that they were not being told to waste money on useless books. But, in contrast to many technologists or scientists who just needed a few quite definite textbooks, the arts and social sciences students often had a range of books recommended for purchase—and they were wary about laying out money for unnecessary books.

'Most lecturers tend to think we print our own money judging by the numbers and costs of the books recommended.' (2nd-year Spanish. £37 spent)

'It would help if the reading lists indicated which books should *definitely* be bought. I have often bought the books suggested and then been told that the department has enough copies to lend out or that I needn't read that book in the original language.' (2nd-year Russian)

'There is little information given about how often a recommended book will be useful during the course.

Books have been bought which prove useful only on one
topic covered, say, in a fortnight.' (2nd-year economics
with mathematics and statistics)

Obviously students are annoyed when they purchase books
which subsequently turn out not to be essential to their courses
and which could just as well be referred to in the library when
needed. The impression given by students is that they are faced
with two problems which overlap, but nevertheless can be
separated. In the case, for example, of languages and law,
students know that they ought to have personal copies of
certain books so that they are on hand all the time and can be
referred to constantly without recourse to the library stock.
In such cases the books are 'tools of the trade' and every
apprentice should collect his own set. But even law students
complain that 'some consideration of expense would contribute
to the value of the guidance given'. Here the student does not
mind buying those books which his lecturers tell him are really
necessary for him to have but, like the student of Spanish, he
does expect his lecturers to give some consideration to his
total annual book expenditure. This is reiterated by a scientist:

'I do not think sufficient emphasis is placed by lecturers
on the cost of books. In my experience many lecturers
assume one's pocket to be bottomless and I would like to
see more medium priced but useful books recommended.'
(2nd-year geology. £25 spent)

Another pure science student does not believe that lecturers
take price into consideration at all when they recommend books
for purchase:

'Lecturers do not keep up to date on prices of any books
they recommend.' (2nd-year zoology)

So there is the problem of how much money students can be
expected to spend in total on books, even if everyone agrees
that certain books really are very desirable for personal possession. On the other hand, there is the second problem, already
commented on, of students being recommended to buy books
which are made to sound as if they are really vital, but then
turn out not to be important at all. This problem seems to be
present in the Faculty of Medicine.

'Book lists often contain expensive, irrelevant books and
omit books which are more useful. One learns of these
by word of mouth from the previous year's students.'
(5th-year medicine)

However, not all students are critical of the quality of advice
given on buying, and one arts student obviously felt that in his
department the staff were both helpful in advice and considerate
of the students' finances:

'Usually it [advice] is good. They [the lecturers] tend to
take into account the fact that with a lot of books to
buy we can't afford always to buy the most expensive.
At the beginning of the year we were given a list of
course books also stating the advised editions to buy.
Since then separate lecturers have advised which books to
read as criticism.' (2nd-year French. Nearly £30 spent)

Lecturers' guidance: general commentary

At the end of the section of the questionnaire dealing with
guidance from lecturers, respondents were asked for any comments which they thought would be helpful. A surprisingly
large 46 per cent of students had no comments to offer at all.
Of those who did offer views, practically one in three wanted
more comments and guidance from their lecturers about the
reading-lists that were distributed. This view was particularly
strongly held by first-year students and those in the fourth year
or over. Also, very interestingly, the first-year students were
well below other years in suggesting that lecturers should
consider the price of books recommended.

Within the eight faculties there were some interesting variations on ideas for improvement. For example, arts students were
less worried about guidance and comments on reading-lists,
whereas in Medicine and Pure Science nearly half the students
offering comments mentioned this point.

Only 3 per cent of medical students felt their lecturers gave
too many references, but 44 per cent of students in Materials
Technology felt theirs did. Book prices seemed particularly
important in the Engineering Faculty, and it was in this faculty
that 13 per cent of comments noted lecturers recommending
their own books too much. Of great interest was the fact that

Table 5.17   General comments on guidance (a)

Please give any comments on the guidance you get from lecturers on reading and book-buying which you feel could be helpful.

	All sample	1st year	2nd year	3rd year	4th year +
No answer	46	46	52	41	47
More guidance/comments on lists	32	37	27	27	47
More guidance on what to buy	16	16	15	19	11
Lecturers give too many references	16	14	16	20	—
Lecturers give too few references	1	—	1	2	—
Lecturers should consider price of books recommended	14	7	19	15	21
Lists given too vague or irrelevant	7	9	9	2	16
Could help by ranking books in importance	6	6	3	8	5
Recommend their own books too much	5	5	7	3	—
More co-ordination between lecturers	3	5	3	3	—
n for comments (excluding no answer) = 100%	295	111	74	91	19

the largest mention of the need for more co-ordination between lecturers came from the Law Faculty. Here there would seem to be a recognition that the best faculty for staff guidance could be even further improved.

I have already put forward a tentative hypothesis about the different ways in which books function in the teaching of various university disciplines. This suggests that in some subjects books themselves are at the heart of the subject and so, in English or French or Spanish, the 'texts' are very much at the core of the teaching. In these subjects students know that certain books must be read and understood if the course is to be tackled at all. Around the core-reading there are critiques and commentaries which allow for a certain freedom

Table 5.18   General comments on guidance (*b*)

	Arts	Soc. Sci.	Arch.	Law	Med.	P.Sci.	Eng.	Mat. Tech.
No answer	42	34	48	39	47	54	48	53
More guidance/ comments on lists	15	29	25	24	48	47	26	22
More guidance on what to buy	15	21	8	24	16	13	16	11
Lecturers give too many references	25	20	25	12	3	9	10	44
Lecturers give too few references	4	—	—	—	3	—	—	—
Lecturers should consider price of books recommended	15	8	8	18	13	14	23	11
Lists given too vague or irrelevant	10	9	17	—	10	5	6	—
Could help by ranking books in importance	8	9	17	12	3	3	—	—
Recommend their own books too much	2	5	—	—	3	6	13	—
More co-ordination between lecturers	6	—	—	12	—	3	6	11
n for comments (excluding 'no answer') = 100%	52	66	12	17	31	77	31	9

of selection and which may not all be read (and certainly not purchased) by even the diligent student. In history and certain descriptive social science subjects such as sociology and politics there are few books which *must* be read. Rather, the lecturers tend to present the students with a range of books for reading and the students are not always told where to begin, or what priorities to give to the many books listed.

Perhaps the important change in subjects comes when we move on to those students who *do* something as well as read about it (and think and talk about it). What I mean here is that many pure scientists, technologists, medicals and dentals spend hours a week in laboratories, practical classes, hospitals and so on. For them, as we have seen, there are explanatory lectures and demonstrations and the *doing* of the subject. This makes sense of the students who explained that they used books to supplement their lectures, as references when they were puzzled by practical tasks, but *not* as the primary sources of information.

For such students as these, the doing of the subject is the crucial activity and 'reading up' about it is an important but nevertheless ancillary activity. This is seen in its most extreme form in the case of some mathematicians and technologists who feel that they are able to 'do' their subjects by attending classes, demonstrations and practical sessions, and that reading about the subject is not necessary at all. The following quotations exemplify these viewpoints, and it should be noted that the students who wrote these comments were simply explaining how their particular courses worked; they were not excusing themselves in any way.

'The lecture notes I take are normally sufficient for my course. Books are only for solving problems in lecture notes or special reference on a particular topic.' (1st-year physics, taking physics, mathematics and computing)

'We are told a few books at the beginning of the year but that's all. However the lecture notes are often, not always, complete in themselves being on the science side.' (2nd-year pure mathematics)

'If the lecturer is of sufficiently high standard books are used for reference purposes only.' (3rd-year mechanical engineering. Nil spent on books)

'Most of my lecturers give rather good lectures resulting in good notes and no need for consulting books.' (3rd-year chemical engineering)

'Providing that one gets all the notes then there is no real need to buy any books at all.' (1st-year materials technology, but £20 spent)

Not every student is satisfied with this situation.

'On my course it tends to be assumed that you can't or won't read but have to be told *everything* in lectures. To pass the exams you just do most of the practice questions [example sheets] given out and your lecture notes contain virtually all you need to do these example sheets.' (2nd-year mechanical engineering)

And a mathematician would have liked to have expanded his thoughts but found the relationship between lectures and books inhibited this:

'In a mathematics course it is important that books reflect the spirit, approach and, where possible, the notation of the lecturing. Otherwise much time can be wasted by the student in reading something which might not be useful to him. Very few of the lecturers make any effort to make their notes compatible with one or two good books. If they did this the student would not only be able to understand the course better but also would have a chance to obtain a far wider and deeper knowledge of his course.' (3rd-year pure mathematics)

Guidance from lecturers to students, then, is varied and can range from excellent to abysmal. As one history student said about reading-lists, 'I feel we are at the mercy of the individual lecturer.' However, good or bad though advice may be about reading, Sheffield University has what is generally acknowledged to be a very good library system. In the next chapter we look closely at undergraduate use of the library.

Chapter 6

Use of university libraries

Introduction

When people talk about study at a university it is often assumed that students spend a great deal of their time working in a library. Such a generalization overlooks the very varied types of courses pursued by undergraduates, some of which are so demanding in hours of class instruction or laboratory work that there is very little time available to the student for private study. The demands upon a student's time are particularly great in the final years of a medical degree, when a student may be attending classes at a number of hospitals and may only rarely go to the university at all. To a lesser extent, students in science and technology may spend many hours on project work in laboratories; architects may work most of their time in the studio. Only in Faculties such as Arts, Social Sciences and Law can it be said that the form of instruction is based upon the expectation that students will have only a limited number of formal classes and a large amount of time in which they are expected to be reading by themselves.

In this chapter we begin by looking at the amount of library usage reported by the students themselves, which includes data on hours spent in classes and in libraries; libraries used for study and for borrowing; and the numbers of books which students have on loan. Attention is then turned to problems which face students in the use of university libraries, and we look at their views on the library stocks in their subjects, difficulties of obtaining references for essays and projects, and the need for multiple copies and books on reserve. Finally we see what suggestions the students themselves are able to offer for improvements in library facilities.

Hours in classes and in libraries

The amount of time which a student spends in classes of various types varies greatly according to the subject or subjects he is studying. In arts or social sciences he may have about eight or nine actual lectures a week, with perhaps another five or six hours in tutorials or seminars. In subjects where laboratory work is an important part of the course, a student may be required to spend several three-hour periods in the laboratory. Choice of subject can thus produce unusual situations, as in the Social Sciences Faculty where a student reading psychology and geography as two of his three first-year subjects would be required to spend an afternoon in laboratory work for each of these two subjects—and this in a faculty which is not generally thought of as being very much associated with laboratory work.

The general university situation is shown in Table 6.1.

Table 6.1 Hours in classes (*a*)

How many hours a week are you normally in
classes of any sort?   ... hours

	All sample	1st year	2nd year	3rd year	4th year +
Up to 9	12	3	13	21	14
10–14	28	29	21	35	11
15–19	18	21	23	12	3
20–24	16	18	22	10	8
25–29	17	24	18	10	13
30 and over	9	5	3	13	53
$n =$	748	263	218	229	38

As this table shows, there are great differences between students in the time which they spend each week in classes of all types. Forty per cent of all students spend under fifteen hours a week in classes, but 26 per cent spend twenty-five hours or more in class. In the normal three-year undergraduate courses, the hours spent in classes are greatest in the first year and gradually decline through the second year to the final year, when 56 per cent have under fifteen hours of classes a week. At the fourth year and beyond, the heavy demands made on medical students result in two-thirds of this group having twenty-five hours or more in classes. The subject differences are brought out in Table 6.2 which gives analysis by faculties.

Table 6.2   Hours in classes (*b*)

	Arts	Soc. Sci.	Arch.	Law	Med.	P.Sci.	Eng.	Mat. Tech.
Up to 9	31	15	41	2	7	5	1	6
10–14	46	50	26	87	5	11	10	6
15–19	18	28	4	11	1	26	11	6
20–24	2	4	7	—	12	26	31	41
25–29	1	1	15	—	32	21	41	34
30 and over	1	—	7	—	42	11	6	6
$n =$	126	118	27	46	78	223	98	32

In Table 6.2 the three main 'book-using' Faculties of Arts, Social Sciences and Law stand out quite distinctly from the other five faculties in the generally small amount of time spent by students each week in formal instruction. Whilst the figure for the social scientists is undoubtedly raised by students reading psychology and geography, for them and for arts and law students only a minority spend fifteen hours or more a week in class. In the Faculty of Architecture, hours in classes vary greatly and the distribution here may have been affected by the way in which some students interpreted the idea of hours in classes, since architecture students frequently spend many hours at their drawing-boards in the departmental studios, though much of this time could be classified as private work rather than formal instruction. In the Faculties of Science, Medicine and Technology there is no such problem of ambiguity, and in all faculties only a minority of undergraduates has less than twenty hours a week of classes, many of them, especially in Medicine, having considerably more.

Given, then, that many students have fairly heavy demands made upon their time by teaching, we may now turn to see how many hours a week these students claim to spend in a university library. Framing this question was not easy, since students do not need to be in a library at all to be doing private study. A student with the appropriate books in his possession, either borrowed or bought, may well prefer to work in his own room rather than in a library. However, it was felt that a question about the amount of time spent in the university libraries would throw some light on the differences between years and faculties in their use of these important university institutions and so, although it must not be misinterpreted to mean more than it does, the question was asked about hours per week in a *university library*. Halls of residence libraries were excluded, because these do not stock curriculum books and are, rather, recreational facilities.

Table 6.3   Hours a week in university library (*a*)

Excluding hall libraries, about how many hours a week do you usually spend in a university library?   ...   hours

	All sample	1st year	2nd year	3rd year	4th year +
None	12	13	10	9	31
Under 5	36	41	33	31	49
5–9	21	25	21	18	9
10–14	14	11	17	15	9
15–19	7	5	6	11	3
20–24	5	2	6	9	—
25–29	4	2	4	5	—
30 and over	2	—	2	3	—
n =	726	257	212	222	35

As Table 6.3 shows, approximately one student in eight in the university does not spend any time in a university library during a normal week, and nearly half of all students spend none or under five hours a week. The previous analysis showed that hours in classes are greatest in the first year and least in the third year of the three-year degree course, and proportions of students spending no time in a university library correspond with this, declining from 13 per cent in the first year to 9 per cent in the third year. Of the fourth-year-and-beyond students, most of whom are medicals, only 21 per cent spend five hours or more a week in a library.

The importance of the type of course being pursued is brought out clearly in Table 6.4.

Table 6.4 Hours a week in university library (*b*)

	Arts	Soc. Sci.	Arch.	Law	Med.	P.Sci.	Eng.	Mat. Tech.
None	4	4	—	2	20	16	19	29
Under 5	13	17	72	11	54	43	54	61
5–9	20	26	16	22	13	25	16	6
10–14	22	16	12	24	10	11	10	—
15–19	15	17	—	13	4	1	—	3
20–24	10	11	—	13	—	3	1	—
25–29	12	3	—	11	—	2	—	—
30 and over	5	4	—	2	—	—	—	—
n =	124	122	25	45	71	214	94	31

There was a 5 per cent non-response to this question, evenly distributed amongst years, but over-proportionately great in the Faculties of Architecture, Medicine and Engineering.

As this table shows, non-use of university libraries is smallest amongst students in the Faculties of Arts, Social Sciences and Law, with Architectural Studies showing a limited use of libraries but very little complete non-use. The Arts and Law Faculties both have 42 per cent of students who use university libraries for fifteen or more hours a week; for the Social Sciences the figure is 35 per cent. Non-usage is greatest in Materials Technology, with only 9 per cent of students claiming a usage of five hours a week or more. In Engineering and Medicine, approximately three-quarters of students spend under five hours a week in a library and for Pure Science the figure is 59 per cent.

Given the type of course being taken and the demands made on their time by formal instruction, the non-use of libraries by scientists and technologists is understandable, but less easy to understand are the 13 per cent of law students, 17 per cent of arts students and 21 per cent of social science students who spend under five hours a week in a university library.

The use of libraries

It has been pointed out that a student may prefer to work in his own room in hall, flat or lodgings rather than in a library provided by the university. There was no question on preferred place of work in the survey, but it was felt that questions on the libraries used for private study and for borrowing of books would be of value. Sheffield University has a very large main library and good-sized branch libraries for applied science and for mathematics, statistics and physics (the Hicks library). Elsewhere there are approximately thirty departmental libraries, some with a full-time assistant (as in law and chemistry) and others, with limited stock and seating, run by enthusiastic academic staff who somehow find time from their teaching and research to run libraries as well.

Tables 6.5 and 6.6 show which libraries students use most for private study, and Tables 6.7 and 6.8 show which libraries they use most for borrowing books.

Table 6.5   Library used for study (*a*)

Which library do you use most for private study?

Name...   None used ☐

	All sample	1st year	2nd year	3rd year	4th year +
None used	15	18	11	14	21
Main university	44	41	44	44	63
Applied science	11	12	13	12	—
*Hicks library	9	13	7	8	—
†Arts Tower departmental	12	11	13	14	3
Other departmental	19	20	21	21	—
Hospital library	1	—	—	—	30
Any others	2	2	2	2	3
n for libraries = 100%	673	225	205	213	30

* Hicks library covers pure mathematics, applied mathematics, physics and computing science.

† The Arts Tower has both arts and social science departmental libraries in it.

As Table 6.5 indicates, 15 per cent of all students say that they do not normally use a library at all for private study and amongst first-year students the figure is 18 per cent. The differences between faculties are more striking than between years, and these are shown below in Table 6.6. Here it can be seen that, in all faculties except Law, Arts and Social Sciences, roughly between a fifth and a quarter of undergraduates do not use libraries at all for private study. The provision of so many departmental libraries in addition to the main library and the two principal branch libraries ensures a diversity of places for work in certain faculties, especially those in Science and Technology.

Table 6.6   Library used for study (*b*)

	Arts	Soc. Sci.	Arch.	Law	Med.	P.Sci.	Eng.	Mat. Tech.
None used	6	7	24	2	19	18	27	25
Main university	56	64	14	7	83	38	17	12
Applied science	—	2	—	—	—	9	60	40
Hicks library	1	1	9	—	—	28	3	—
Arts Tower departmental	42	10	73	—	—	—	—	—
Other departmental	2	22	—	93	—	22	13	36
Hospital library	—	—	—	—	14	—	1	—
Public library	—	1	5	—	—	—	—	—
Hall library	—	—	—	—	—	1	—	4
Any others	—	1	—	—	—	3	6	8
n for libraries = 100%	127	119	22	45	64	193	78	25

Reasons for choosing one library in which to work in preference to another were very interesting. A first-year French, Spanish and English student who used the main library wrote:

> 'The departmental libraries are totally impossible to work in. They seem to be more like social centres for coffee and talk than a place to study in.'

But a second-year student of English felt differently:

'It is impossible to work in the railway-station atmosphere
of the main reading-room [main library]. I am lucky to
have the English Department library to work in.'

Another first-year arts student reading politics, history and
economic history disliked the large reading-room of the main
library:

'I find the somewhat crowded and noisy conditions of the
main library difficult and I prefer the quieter History
departmental library. Perhaps carpeted floors might help
to reduce the noise problem.'

But a third-year French student was of the opinion that
'Departmental libraries are frequently very noisy, but this is
obviously the students' own fault.'

Perhaps the right conclusion from such comments is that
some choice between large and small reading-rooms is desirable,
since students do vary considerably in the size of library they
prefer.

Other comments about the working environment introduced
some novel and even unexpected ideas. A third-year student
in medicine wanted facilities where students could work in
pairs or groups. A third-year dental student wanted more desks
and chairs to be placed in the book-stacks—places where a few
seats have been introduced only because of shortage of space.
Partitions down the centres of the tables in the main library
(as provided in the applied science library) were wanted by an
electrical engineer, and a third-year arts student complained
of over-heating in the main library reading-room and stacks.

A first-year student in the integrated biology course wrote,
'Students should be allowed to take their own books into the
library to do private study.' This student is, of course, completely wrong in believing that there is an embargo on this.
Brief-cases are not allowed in the library, but there is no
prohibition at all on personal books.

Departmental libraries came in for some criticism. An
architecture student commented that his library was closed
at lunch-time and after 5 p.m., which greatly limited his access
to it. A zoology student complained that, as an undergraduate,
he was not allowed to use the physiology departmental library,
and another zoologist said that undergraduates were not able
to use the zoology library.

Perhaps the most pitiful comment of all was from a first-year student of politics, psychology and sociology: 'The prohibition on smoking limits the time I can spend in the library.'

Whilst Tables 6.5 and 6.6 show the amount of use made of libraries for private study, no mention has yet been made of the lending function of the libraries. All students were asked what library they used most for borrowing books and, as Table 6.7 shows, 16 per cent of all students, approximately one in every six, said they did not use any library (including public libraries) for borrowing books.

Table 6.7   Library used for borrowing (*a*)

Which library do you use most for borrowing books?

Name...   None used ☐

	All sample	1st year	2nd year	3rd year	4th year +
None used	16	25	13	8	21
Main university	53	54	50	50	83
Applied science	14	14	15	16	—
Hicks library	6	6	6	6	—
Arts Tower departmental	7	8	6	7	3
Other departmental	15	14	16	18	3
Hospital library	—	—	—	—	7
Public library	2	2	3	1	3
Hall library	1	—	2	—	—
Any others	2	2	3	1	—
n for libraries = 100%	666	209	199	229	29

Once again non-usage of the library is highest amongst first-year students, less in the second year, and at its lowest in the third year. The category of fourth-year-and-over again reflects the practice of medical students. It may come as a surprise that a quarter of all first-year students claim not to use any library at all for borrowing books. This could be a reflection of high buying of books amongst these students, which makes borrowing unnecessary, or it may be that in certain degree courses the need for borrowing books is minimal.

The faculty analysis in Table 6.8 would appear to support the latter hypothesis.

Table 6.8   Library used for borrowing (*b*)

	Arts	Soc. Sci.	Arch.	Law	Med.	P.Sci.	Eng.	Mat. Tech.
None used	5	7	—	13	26	27	13	28
Main university	78	80	33	10	89	47	3	4
Applied science	—	2	—	—	—	10	64	78
Hicks library	1	1	3	—	—	19	2	—
Arts Tower departmental	16	3	60	—	2	1	1	—
Other departmental	1	8	—	90	2	18	24	4
Hospital library	—	—	—	—	4	—	—	—
Public library	2	4	3	—	4	1	—	4
Hall library	—	—	—	—	—	3	—	—
Any others	2	1	—	—	—	2	5	9
n for libraries = 100%	132	121	30	42	57	174	87	23

Table 6.8 shows that, whilst 16 per cent of all students do not borrow books from any library, the figures for the Faculties of Medicine, Pure Science and Materials Technology exceed a quarter of students. It was expected from previous data that engineering students would have been with these three faculties but, for reasons not known, this was not so. Non-borrowing amongst law students, at 13 per cent, might be considered high for them, though it should be appreciated that in this subject a great deal of *reference* work is carried out in the library without necessarily *borrowing* the books, some of which may not even be available for loan. Again, though, it is surprising that one in twenty of arts students and one in fourteen of social science students are able to follow their courses without needing to borrow any books.

Several comments made by students showed that there were problems encountered in borrowing from libraries, especially as departmental libraries not under direct university-library control are able to make their own regulations, which may even preclude borrowing.

'All departmental libraries ought to lend out books, at least overnight.' (2nd-year French)

'Often books are kept out of departmental libraries for much longer than the maximum of one week since there is no way of enforcing this.' (1st-year arts)

'Books from the Chemistry library can only be borrowed overnight and this is not always enough for books recommended to us by the lecturers.' (3rd-year chemistry)

'In the Department of Geology a lot of books cannot be removed from the library or department and this makes it difficult to work at home.' (2nd-year geology)

'It is possible to remove books from the Law library without filling in any forms. These surrupticious [*sic*] removals have become very common.' (3rd-year law)

The matter of borrowing books was taken further by a particular question which asked each student how many books he (or she) had on loan from the library (or libraries) at that time. The response came as a shock to the author, as over a third of all undergraduates replied that they had no books on loan from the library at a point just after halfway through the Lent Term. As Table 6.9 shows, the 'first- to third-year' gradation was again found, and over 40 per cent of first-year students said they had no book on loan from the library at the time of the survey. Looking at those students who had *most* books out from the various libraries, 28 per cent of third-year students had five or more books on loan compared with 17 per cent of second-years and 16 per cent of first-years.

Not unexpectedly, the analysis of book-borrowing by faculties (Table 6.10) brought out some interesting differences. The faculty with the highest percentage of students with no books on loan was Law. Other survey data can be used to demonstrate that law students are the best book *buyers* in the university and, as the previous Tables 6.4, 6.6 and 6.8 have shown, they are high library users. Clearly, then, law students use their library very much as a reference library rather than as a lending library. However, in both Medicine and Pure Science half the students have no university books out on loan and here the position is different from that of Law. Medical students do

Table 6.9   Books on loan (a)

How many university books have you out now?				... books
	All sample	1st year	2nd year	3rd year	4th year +
None	35	41	36	25	51
1	11	11	9	11	16
2	14	16	15	12	14
3	9	9	10	8	14
4	11	7	12	15	3
5	10	7	10	14	3
6	3	3	2	4	—
7	2	1	2	2	—
8	1	—	1	3	—
9	1	2	—	1	—
10 or more	3	3	2	4	—
$n =$	737	258	214	228	37

need to buy books for their course and they are the second highest book-buyers after law students. Pure scientists, however, are not (as future data will show) great book-buyers, and it may be suggested that certain courses in pure science require little use of books at all—so that use of the library for study or borrowing is at a fairly low level.

About a third of engineers and materials technologists have no books on loan, which again may indicate courses in which a few textbooks, perhaps purchased, may be adequate for students. Architecture students are said to use a large number of reports and pamphlets, which may account for their 22 per cent with no books on loan. More surprising are the 10 per cent of arts students and 20 per cent of social science students with no books on loan. In these faculties, where breadth of reading is so often expected, these would seem to be very sizeable minorities.

So far the tables in this chapter have dealt only with factual information supplied by the students. However, their views on the problems which face them in making use of the university library facilities are equally important, and these opinions are dealt with in the next section.

Table 6.10 Books on loan (b)

	Arts	Soc. Sci.	Arch.	Law	Med.	P.Sci.	Eng.	Mat. Tech.
None	10	20	22	52	50	51	34	37
1	5	8	19	19	20	8	13	23
2	10	20	19	7	9	15	20	3
3	13	8	19	2	9	4	15	20
4	20	15	7	7	4	9	7	3
5	20	17	7	2	5	6	7	3
6	6	4	4	2	—	2	1	7
7	6	2	—	—	—	1	—	3
8	2	2	4	—	—	1	—	—
9	2	2	—	2	1	—	1	—
10 or more	7	3	—	5	—	3	1	—
$n =$	124	120	27	42	74	221	99	30

Problems in using the libraries

As consumers of the libraries provided for them, undergraduates are in an important position to assess the book stocks in the

Table 6.11 Opinion on library stock (a)

In general do you consider the university library stock in your subject(s) is:

Very good; Fairly good; So-so; Fairly poor; Very poor?

	All sample	1st year	2nd year	3rd year	4th year +
Very good	10	11	7	8	29
Fairly good	45	50	41	46	32
So-so	26	24	26	30	24
Fairly poor	13	12	18	12	8
Very poor	5	3	8	4	8
$n =$	733	249	216	230	38
Score	60	64	55	61	67

K

libraries. A general question was therefore put to them, asking
what they thought of the library stock in their subject or
subjects. As Table 6.11 demonstrates, opinion, on the whole,
was favourable rather than unfavourable, with 55 per cent of
all students on the 'good' side and only 18 per cent on the 'poor'
side. First-year students and fourth-year-and-over students
were more favourably inclined than were second- or third-year
students (though it might be noted that the two former groups
were the smallest users of libraries).

Amongst the eight faculties the law students were most
satisfied with their library stock and only in the Faculties of
Medicine and Engineering did more than 20 per cent of students
feel that their stock was poor.

Table 6.12   Opinion on library stock (b)

	Arts	Soc. Sci.	Arch.	Law	Med.	P.Sci.	Eng.	Mat. Tech.
Very good	8	5	14	29	15	9	6	13
Fairly good	50	45	38	47	39	43	48	48
So-so	28	31	34	18	24	27	21	26
Fairly poor	9	13	14	4	15	14	20	13
Very poor	5	6	—	2	8	6	5	—
n =	128	122	29	45	75	207	96	31
Score	60	58	63	74	60	58	58	65

There were a lot of comments from respondents about book
stocks, though surprisingly few from the social scientists. Many
students commented on the uselessness of old and out-of-date
books in the libraries. This criticism came especially from
students in the biological sciences:

'I can only speak for biology books, but my impression
is that most of the books are too out-dated, some of
them being 30–40 years old with completely wrong ideas,
and there are no alternative newer books.' (1st-year
integrated biology)

'Generally the books relevant to my course are out of

date, or perhaps the new ones are very quickly snapped up.' (2nd-year zoology, botany and physiology)

'Some books in the sciences tend to be out of date and new ones would be useful, that is editions after 1970.' (2nd-year biochemistry)

'The Geology journals are very good but Geology books are often irrelevant and out of date.' (3rd-year geology)

An impression came from students in the Faculty of Medicine of a lot of out-dated dead stock on their library shelves. This was very forcibly put by one fifth-year student:

'The supply of medical texts on the general shelves [that is not on reserve] is lamentable. There are inadequate duplicate copies and the vast majority of popular texts are out of date. It should be noted that any medical book more than about five years old is out of date. Many of those on the library shelves are fifteen to twenty years old and useless.'

The uselessness of out-dated texts was echoed by a fifth-year dentistry student:

'Have modern text books, not old ones with out-of-date theories and ideas now known to be wrong.'

A second-year medical student who rarely used the library said that too many books were very old and thus useless to him and he wanted 'some good books around to arouse interest'. Because of this lack he did not use the library much.

But biology and medicine were not alone in the criticisms. A first-year student in arts was quite vituperative in commenting:

'You could destroy all the Roman history books because even the lecturers say they are useless, out of date and boring.'

A rather more polite student of English wrote:

'An improvement in the English Language section of the Main library would be appreciated.'

Comments on out-of-date books were made also by students in the Faculties of Civil Engineering and Metallurgy, and law students commented on the inadequacy of the stock of their library as well as it being over-crowded for users.

In addition to the general question on stock, student respondents were asked a specific question about difficulties in obtaining books for their essays or project work. This question deals more specially with inadequacy of numbers of *copies* of books, rather than the *quality* of the general stock, and replies showed that over half the undergraduates did have problems.

Table 6.13 Obtaining books for essays, etc. (*a*)

Do you have difficulty in getting books in the library for essays or projects for your courses?

Very much; Fairly much; So-so; Not much; None at all

	All sample	1st year	2nd year	3rd year	4th year +
Very much	28	28	32	25	21
Fairly much	27	26	27	31	16
So-so	17	16	22	14	16
Not much	20	19	16	22	42
None at all	7	10	4	8	5
$n =$	713	237	211	227	38
Score	62	60	67	61	52

Table 6.13 is interesting as showing that, whilst differences between first-, second- and third-years are not very great, it is the second- and third-years who have slightly more difficulty than the first- and fourth-year students in obtaining books, and it was the second- and third-year students who had the less favourable views on book stocks in Table 6.11.

When we look at the analyses by faculty, those of Arts and Social Sciences both have very high 'problem scores' compared with other faculties, and these are two faculties which conventionally require a great deal of essay writing, based on broad reading, from the students.

Table 6.14 Obtaining books for essays, etc. (b)

	Arts	Soc. Sci.	Arch.	Law	Med.	P.Sci.	Eng.	Mat. Tech.
Very much	43	48	3	26	19	23	11	7
Fairly much	32	30	31	37	14	23	31	23
So-so	16	15	17	11	13	17	28	20
Not much	9	6	38	20	42	24	24	30
None at all	2	1	10	4	12	13	6	20
$n =$	129	122	29	46	69	198	90	30
Score	77	80	44	64	47	55	54	42

There was a large number of comments from arts and social science students about the problems of obtaining the books they needed, and many of these comments noted the problems arising from the liberal borrowing regulations of the university library. It may be useful to note here that an undergraduate is allowed five books from the main library to be held until the end of term unless they are recalled because another reader requests them. A borrower may hold any book for a minimum of a week, but if requested to return it he must do this within three days in term-time (one week in vacation) or be fined 5p for each day a book is overdue. Theoretically, therefore, any book on loan is obtainable within ten days *if requested*, but very few students indeed use this reservation scheme (or even appear to be aware of it). As a result, students complain bitterly about the long loan period allowed for books and advocate a shortening of it. This is often associated in students' views with the desirability of books actually being on the *shelves* in the library so that people can see them when browsing. The point is made by a third-year student of English, history and pre-history:

'Reduce the loan period—a term is far too long. Unless the reader has heard of a book he need never know that it exists or that it is available because it never appears on the shelves from term to term.'

The tendency to borrow books and not bother to return them is noted by a third-year student of French and Russian:

'Books should not be on loan for a whole term at a time.
There is a tendency to borrow a book which one thinks
might later be needed and return it at the end of term
without having opened it.'

Views on a suitable loan period varied. A first-year student
of economics, sociology and law advocated a period of only
one week, whilst a first-year student reading English and
politics wanted three weeks because that was the period of loan
from the public library.

Skill in assessing when to recall a book on loan was obviously
lacking in one student:

'A quicker calling in of books which you reserve and need
for essays. They usually arrive after you have handed
in the essay.' (2nd-year history)

But a first-year arts student felt that it was the duty of the
staff to stop the books being borrowed at all:

'Tutors should have special books for essays put on
temporary reserve before they set the essays.'

This recommendation has some sense if the tutor does know
what *special* books will be needed and when they will be needed,
but not every tutor is so well organized. Problems of access to
books cannot be wholly overcome by putting them on temporary reserve, since this leads students to complain that they
are restricted to using them in the library. There is no simple
solution to the problem of many students having reasonable
access to very limited copies of a book.

But other problems than these do occur. A third-year history
student noted that 'important books and periodicals disappear
without trace' and a first-year student of psychology, sociology
and philosophy pointed out that if students removed journals
from the stacks and left them on the reading-room tables no
one else could find them until the next day when the staff had
collected, sorted and replaced them.

Pilfering of single copies of journals was a problem for some
medical students who could not find copies of the *British
Medical Journal* or the *Lancet*, and a third-year zoology student
went so far as to suggest that *all* periodicals should be restricted
to the library.

Certainly there was a strong impression of too many students chasing too few books. This was reinforced by replies to a question asking students if lack of multiple copies of books created any difficulties for them.

Table 6.15   Lack of multiple copies (*a*)

Do you have any difficulty because of lack of multiple copies of particular books?

Very much; Fairly much; So-so; Not much; None at all

	All sample	1st year	2nd year	3rd year	4th year +
Very much	38	36	42	38	27
Fairly much	25	26	26	24	27
So-so	14	16	13	11	16
Not much	14	11	14	18	14
None at all	8	11	5	8	16
n =	726	242	217	230	37
Score	67	66	72	66	59

As Table 6.15 indicates, nearly two-thirds of all students say they have either 'fairly much' or 'very much' difficulty because of the lack of multiple copies of books in their subjects. This response cannot, of course, simply be taken at its face value as an edict to the library to spend all its money on buying multiple copies of undergraduate books. We have already seen that students *could* make better use of the recall system and we shall, in the next chapter, see that they could spend more money on purchasing books. But student demand for multiple copies does seem quite clear, and it would seem to be particularly a problem in the 'bookish' Faculties of Arts and Social Sciences, as Table 6.16 shows.

The 'problem scores' of eighty-five for Social Sciences and eighty-one for Arts are very high ones, and come from at least four out of every five students saying that they have 'fairly' or 'very' much of a problem in these Faculties. There is also quite a large problem in Law, but the other five faculties all have a

Table 6.16   Lack of multiple copies (*b*)

	Arts	Soc. Sci.	Arch.	Law	Med.	P.Sci.	Eng.	Mat. Tech.
Very much	53	59	24	41	30	29	22	31
Fairly much	28	29	28	28	19	25	24	21
So-so	9	6	17	13	18	15	24	7
Not much	8	6	17	13	18	18	23	17
None at all	2	1	14	4	15	13	9	24
n =	129	121	29	46	73	206	93	29
Score	81	85	58	72	58	60	58	55

score within the range fifty-five to sixty, and, rather surprisingly, the Medical Faculty is not particularly different from the others, although one third-year medical student did comment:

'There is usually only one copy of a medical book and perhaps 80 students after that copy.'

This point of very large numbers of students is repeated by an arts student:

'Some lecturers set one essay for 60 pupils. If the books are not on reserve, which usually they are not, the situation is hopeless.' (3rd-year history and politics)

A very interesting variation of the theme came from a second-year accountancy student who wanted 'More modern books and more multiple copies so that the lecturers and tutors are unable to take out all the relevant and useful books as happens at present'. It is interesting to see that this accountancy student does not consider how easy it would be to *recall* these books from the lecturers simply by reserving them at the library counter.

A first-year student of English and economic history wanted more multiple copies of texts and criticisms and considered that 'a Reserve Book Room is an excuse for buying no more copies of a popular book.'

Just how far the university library should go in for providing multiple copies of what are often quite expensive undergraduate texts is no easy problem to resolve. There is always a problem in allocating scarce resources and, as any librarian knows, the *possible* expenditure for a university library has no theoretical limits.

A danger is that, with the unfilled demand for multiple copies, the copyright laws will be deliberately broken by photo-copying. At present, library users are allowed one personal copy of an article or *short* extract from a book, but there is a clear and dangerous attraction in the idea of photo-copying whole chapters of books (or even whole books if they are very expensive) and if this is permitted then publishers will rightly complain of such piracy.

As one practical way of trying to provide access to much-needed books, Sheffield University main library has a Reserve-book Collection housed quite separately from the general stocks and reading-room. At the time of the survey in 1972 this reserve was housed in the main library building and numbered about 1,000 volumes. Since then it has been rehoused on the first floor of the adjacent arts building and now has seating for a hundred people and shelving for several thousand volumes if necessary.

In theory a Reserve-book Room, Much-used-book Collection, or Undergraduate Collection has much to commend it. No matter how much demand there is for a book, the Reserve Collection will have one copy which is generally available and may, at most, only be borrowed from late afternoon until early morning. As a *practical* way of trying to provide maximum use of much-wanted books it is clearly as much as a library can offer. All students were therefore asked how many times during the current Lent Term they had made use of this library facility. As Table 6.17 shows, just over a third of all students had used it.

Differences between the years of study were not very great, though it was interesting to see that students in the fourth year and above had made slightly more use of the room than others, indicating that medical students had found some use in it. Use by different faculties varied considerably as Table 6.18 shows.

This table must be read carefully, since the Reserve-book Room is situated in the main library and there is a major branch library at the St George's Square site half a mile away,

Table 6.17   Use of Reserve-book Room (*a*)

So far this term (since Christmas) how many times have you used a
book in the main library Reserve-book Room?   ...   times

	All sample	1st year	2nd year	3rd year	4th year +
None	65	67	61	68	53
Once	7	7	6	6	11
Twice	7	8	8	3	11
3 times	4	3	5	5	5
4 times	3	2	4	3	8
5 times	1	1	3	1	—
6–9 times	4	4	4	4	5
10–14 times	4	4	5	2	3
15–19 times	1	1	1	2	3
20 or more	4	2	2	6	3
n =	709	247	205	219	38

Table 6.18   Use of Reserve-book Room (*b*)

	Arts	Soc. Sci.	Arch.	Law	Med.	P.Sci.	Eng.	Mat. Tech.
None	41	25	74	72	44	85	96	100
Once	11	11	13	—	7	5	3	—
Twice	11	9	9	15	9	4	—	—
3 times	8	10	—	8	7	1	—	—
4 times	4	8	4	3	5	1	—	—
5 times	3	3	—	3	3	—	—	—
6–9 times	5	11	—	—	9	1	1	—
10–14 times	8	10	—	—	5	1	—	—
15–19 times	3	2	—	—	5	—	—	—
20 or more	7	11	—	—	5	—	—	—
n =	119	116	23	39	75	213	96	28

There was a 7 per cent non-response to this question, evenly distributed
amongst years but over-proportionately great in the Faculties of
Architecture, Law and Materials Technology.

catering for engineering and materials technology. Law and architecture both have highly specialized departmental libraries, and the Hicks library is situated in a building used by mathematics, physics, statistics and computing. Use of the Reserve-book Room would thus be expected to be dominated by students in arts, social sciences and medicine and some subjects of pure science. Even here, though, it must be remembered that many arts departments run their own libraries, and so expectation of usage is very difficult to assess. What Table 6.18 does show is an interesting pattern of usage amongst social science students and to a lesser degree in arts and medicine. However, a Reserve-book Room is very much what members of staff make it, and some comments from students give interesting perspectives on this.

A first-year medical student actually complained:

'Too many relevant books for my course are placed in the
Reserve Book Room, thus making them difficult to
obtain except by working in the library.'

This student does not say whether the books he wants are *only* in the Reserve Collection; in fact many books on reserve (especially those on permanent reserve) are duplicate copies, and at least one copy is always available for long-term loan. In complete contrast to the medical student a third-year history student advocated

'Expand the Reserve-book Room. I would use it but it
often does not contain what I want.'

A second-year psychology student wanted more use to be made of this collection for temporary reserve:

'More books should be put on reserve when a class has a
set project or essays to do, as there is no time to recall
a book that is out on loan and read it for an essay which
has to be completed in a fortnight.'

This student has a valid point, but if his wishes were to be met the lecturer setting the essay would have to communicate his intentions in very good time to the librarian in charge of the Reserve-book Room so that she could recall the necessary books out on loan and classify and catalogue them specially for the Reserve Collection. This need not take too much time if the people holding books returned them promptly when they were recalled, but no lecturer (or student) should expect an overnight service for requests for books to be put on temporary reserve.

A number of students obviously wanted some form of very short-term loan which would allow them to remove books from the library even if only for '4 to 24 hours', as one history student put it. In fact, books may be borrowed overnight from the Reserve-book Room as long as they are not taken out more than half an hour before closing and are returned the next day before 9.30 a.m. Few students, however, appear to have read the *Reader's Guide to the Library* which gives this useful information.

Some students had noticed differences in the stocks of various subjects in the Reserve Collection:

'I found when I studied history that the Reserve Book Room was very useful, but there are hardly any English course books in it.' (3rd-year English)

'French lecturers should be encouraged to place books in heavy demand in the Reserve Book Room.' (2nd-year French)

Yet both these students of English and French have good-sized *departmental* libraries run specially for them; so clearly there is a lack of *policy* about what books are needed, rather than just a lack of stock.

In the law library, where many books are kept on reserve or restricted to overnight loan, there appear to be some students who abuse the service:

'A better check should be kept on reference books. In the Law library books allowed out of the library overnight are very often kept out for over a week.' (1st-year law)

Quite a number of students had recommendations which brought together a more limited *general* loan period and a slight extension of the *reserve* stock period. Ideas of one or two weeks for general borrowing and two or three days for reserve borrowing were not uncommon. What students clearly do not appreciate is that such short periods necessitate a great deal of clerical work in recalling books held over the given time-period, and in 1972–3 the Deputy Librarian estimated that two full-time assistants would be needed to implement shorter loan periods. It is hoped that computerization will eventually replace the laborious hand-filed borrowing-slips in use at present.

One very interesting positive suggestion for improvement came from a third-year student of pure mathematics. He wrote:

'It would be a good idea if the books recommended for buying at the beginning of courses were made temporary reference books so that people could judge whether they would find them useful.'

Anyone can, of course, browse through books in the bookshop but it might well be that the easier access to such books via the Reserve Collection could stimulate some students to buy for themselves.

As the above quotations have demonstrated, some students are capable of making interesting and constructive suggestions about the use of books in the university libraries. The final section of this chapter deals with general library suggestions offered by students.

Suggestions for improvements to the library services

It will be recalled that in the communication model given on page 5 there is one possible line of communication from the student to the lecturer. This means that it is possible for a student to pass useful information about books to his lecturers. It may be less common than the communication from lecturer to student, since the lecturer is the more experienced person whose duty it is to instruct the student.

It was felt that a useful question in the survey could ask students if they had ever suggested a book for the library to any lecturer. The question was framed:

'Have you ever suggested to a lecturer a book that you think ought to be in the library?'   Yes;   No.

Six students did not answer this question, and of the 757 who did answer 68 said 'yes', which is 9 per cent of the total respondents.

As Table 6.19 shows, there is a slight increase from first- to third-year, and both the third-year and fourth-year-and-beyond

Table 6.19   Suggestions to lecturers

The distribution of the 68 by year was:

			%	Survey sample %
1st-year	10	=	15	35
2nd-year	19	=	28	29
3rd-year	34	=	50	31
4th-year +	5	=	7	5
	68		100	100

The distribution by faculty was:

			%	Survey sample %
Arts	14	=	21	17
Soc. Sci.	19	=	28	16
Arch.	3	=	4	4
Law	4	=	6	6
Med.	4	=	6	10
P. Sci.	12	=	18	30
Eng.	8	=	12	13
Mat. Tech.	4	=	6	4
	68		100	100

groups are above their proportions in the general sample. Analysis by faculty gives arts and social science students proportions above 'par' and especially is this so for the social scientists. Materials technology students also come slightly above expectation. Generally speaking, though, this is an aspect of communication which is not used very much, and only one arts student wrote a comment saying that he thought the library should 'provide for suggestions for new books either by book or box'.

The final question in the section of the survey dealing with the use of the library asked students for suggestions for improving the library service. Tables 6.20 and 6.21 analyse these suggestions and it will be seen that nearly half of all the respondents had no suggestions at all to offer—a surprising lack of response from a body of people who have in recent years been prepared to take militant action to have their views listened to by university authorities, though, it must be conceded, the student body in Sheffield has not been noted for its support of physical violence in backing up its arguments.

Table 6.20   Suggestions for library improvement (*a*)

Please give any suggestions for the improvement of the university library service.

	All sample	1st year	2nd year	3rd year	4th year +
No answer	47	55	45	39	50
More multiple copies	25	28	26	24	14
More books on reserve	21	16	26	21	21
Reduce or limit loan period	19	19	23	15	7
Improve departmental libraries	9	14	7	8	—
More new editions of books	8	8	12	4	21
Improve security/reduce stealing	5	5	1	8	14
Restrict loans of journals	4	2	1	8	14
Improve seating	4	4	1	6	14
Better staff/library co-operation	2	2	2	3	—
More/better library instruction	1	3	1	1	—
n (excluding 'no answer') =	419	112	137	156	14

The proportions of students offering no suggestions at all decline from 55 per cent in the first year to 39 per cent in the third year, but rise again to 50 per cent for the fourth-year-and-above group.

Those improvements which receive most attention are concerned primarily with accessibility of books; multiple copies, more reserve books and reduced loan periods receive far more attention than anything else. It is interesting to note that 5 per cent of suggestions were concerned with problems of security and prevention of theft. The need for better staff/library co-operation and improved library instruction for students received very little attention, and this must reflect the lack of knowledge on the part of students of the underlying human factors which can make or mar a good library. Sadly, it would appear that the students know so little about using a library well that they do not even appreciate how uninstructed they are.

The analysis by faculties is given in Table 6.21, where the greater interest of students in Social Sciences, Arts and Law is apparent.

Table 6.21   Suggestions for library improvement (*b*)

	Arts	Soc. Sci.	Arch.	Law	Med.	P.Sci.	Eng.	Mat. Tech.
No answer	33	24	52	33	49	59	60	66
More multiple copies	28	19	—	38	29	24	29	40
More books on reserve	23	34	8	10	18	17	14	10
Reduce or limit loan period	20	24	17	14	6	18	21	10
Improve departmental libraries	11	3	42	17	—	14	—	10
More new editions of books	6	3	8	7	21	11	14	10
Improve security/ reduce stealing	2	6	—	12	3	4	7	10
Restrict loans of journals	1	7	8	—	6	6	4	—
Improve seating	4	2	17	2	18	1	4	—
Better staff/ library co-operation	3	2	—	—	—	4	4	—
More/better library instruction	1	2	—	—	—	1	4	10
n (excluding 'no answer') =	90	107	12	42	34	96	28	10

Law students are eager to have more multiple copies of books but are not great supporters of books on reserve or of reduced loan periods. By contrast, the social scientists are keen on reserved books and reduced loan periods, but do not support more multiple copies as much. These differences probably reflect the different needs and ways of study of the two groups.

Medical students are rather concerned about out-of-date editions of books, and law students are the most concerned about book-stealing and security. Perhaps it is appropriate that the two groups of students most concerned about improved seating are the architects and the medicals.

Overall, however, the interests of the students as reflected in their suggestions showed a very limited and unsophisticated appreciation of library facilities and possibilities. Suggestions for reader services and information-retrieval were conspicuously absent. There were requests for a better guide to the indexing system from a first-year social scientist. A first-year geographer wanted the main library to have 'a separate catalogue for articles in periodicals classified by subject as the Geographical Association Library [in Sheffield] does', but he could not appreciate what a mammoth task this would be for every subject and journal in the university. A medical student wanted further subject divisions within the field of medicine, and a social scientist wanted better *subject* labelling of stacks rather than merely Dewey numbers. The time required to complete borrowing-slips was adversely commented on by a third-year electrical engineer who preferred the public-library ticket system. Medical students would have liked to have had access late on Saturdays and on Sundays, as their clinical training gave them little time in the week for library study. Students from a number of faculties commented on problems of theft and on students who hide books and journals (especially those not allowed to be borrowed) in obscure corners of the library. And, inevitably, there were a few adverse comments about the counter-staff, though these were actually very few and not much worse than the comment of the technologist who wrote, 'Tell the girls behind the counter to be a bit more cheerful. A smile never does any harm'.

As this chapter has shown, there are considerable differences between students in their use of university library facilities, and a fair-sized minority seems to be able to pursue its studies quite happily with very little help from the libraries. Of course, if each student has a good personal library, he may not need to borrow very much.

In the next chapter we look at students and their relationships with bookshops.

L

Chapter 7

Students and bookshops

Introduction

Educational booksellers in Britain are not infrequently heard to bemoan a system of school education in this country which, coupled with an excellent public-library system, offers no incentive to young people to purchase books for themselves. While at school the young person is provided, at no cost to himself, with all the basic books he requires for his courses. If he needs extra books, his school library or his local public library are at hand to meet his needs.

By contrast, European countries, especially Scandinavian countries, tend more to a system where school books must be bought by the pupils, and public library provision is not too generous. In these countries the purchase of school books may consist of little more than presenting the local bookseller with a standard list and receiving a package of books, but, as booksellers in Britain point out, the parents and the children do become conditioned to *buying* books for educational purposes and the step to buying books at university is merely a progression along the same lines.

In Britain the step becomes more of a jump—and often rather a jump in the dark. Having been previously required to buy virtually nothing, the first-year university student is suddenly placed in a position of having a nominal sum of £48 (1971–2 session) in his grant for the purchase of 'books, equipment and materials'. Since this amount is not specially set aside in the form of book vouchers, the student must decide for himself how to apportion his expenditure so as to use his grant most wisely over the twelve-month period. The 'other common elements (nominal)' described by the Department of Education and Science for the year 1971–2 were £42 for vacation spending, £15 for travel (other than additional allowances for travel between university and home each term and from lodgings to university each day), £48 for pocket money, and £45 for clothes, laundry and dry-cleaning. These nominal sums add up to £198 and, together with the lodgings allowance of £232, make a total of £430 for the year for the university student at a provincial university. For students at any higher-education college in London or at the universities of Oxford or Cambridge the lodging sum was £267; for students living at home it was £147.

The main point in the above details is that, no matter where the student lives, he receives money for a number of standard nominal elements, amongst which books are specially mentioned. From the very outset, therefore, the new student knows that he is expected to spend money on books. What he spends the money on and how much he spends will depend greatly upon the guidance given to him by his lecturers. If, as is very common at university, his first-year course is made up of several different subjects, he may well have to take careful decisions as to how to apportion his money between the different subjects. It would be easy to say that, for a three-subject first year, £12 should be spent on each subject, but such an egalitarian approach might well ignore the differences of book requirements between the subjects.

Moving from the theoretical to the harsh practicalities of life, the student may have to look into the 'nominal common elements' for subsidies if his lodgings and meals cost him more than £7.73 per week. If it becomes apparent to him that it is not essential to spend money on books, then the student may well decide to use that £48 for other things. It is very difficult to make any generalizations about the way in which students spend their grant, since no impartial surveys of this topic have been published, and statements from the National Union of Students are, understandably, partisan. Nevertheless, it does seem clear that many parents who are assessed by their local authorities for contributions to their sons' and daughters' grants do not make up the difference between the amount given to the student by the local authority and the standard annual maintenance rates. With only a notional £430 a year to live on, any student whose parent does not make up the difference must clearly be in dire straits. A further point rarely mentioned is that students of most universities are on vacation for twenty-two weeks of the year, and there is no board-and-lodgings allowance for this period. It is quite clear from the £42 'vacation allowance' that parents are expected to provide board and lodgings free in the vacations. If this were not so, the £147 board and lodgings allowance for students living at home during term would result in a comparable £107.80 for the vacations. Students are, not unnaturally, reluctant to see themselves in the role of objects of domestic charity for twenty-two weeks of the year, and so vacation jobs away from home become attractive as means of earning money to top up the grant, as well as reducing dependency on parents. The lack of desire to be at home during vacations has in recent years been increased, not only by normal feelings of independence, but also by greater numbers of students living in flats or bed-sitters where rents have to be paid all the year round, and by an increase in the numbers of students given vacation grants for personal study rather than for organized field-courses.

All these factors, complex though they may be, and at times seemingly far removed from the purchase of books, nevertheless do come together to produce a situation in which the modern student has to make careful decisions about his annual expenditure if he is to remain solvent. That some students seem to be able to include running motorcars, smoking, and drinking in their budgets may be surprising, but we do not know how much these luxuries are paid for by many weeks of dreary employment throughout the three vacations. What was clear from some replies in the Sheffield survey was that a minority of students, 4 per cent overall, do not buy books.

As one first-year student reading Economics, Accountancy and Sociology put it, 'I've not bought any books yet.'

Replies in the section dealing with bookshops and the purchase of books were not always very logical, but in many instances they were nevertheless very enlightening. To say that book prices are high is not surprising, but to say that you have spent *nothing* at all on books over the year *because* of high prices is not a very logical argument. Yet it seemed to satisfy one student.

In this chapter we begin by considering the students' use of bookshops in Sheffield and then go on to consider the students' book-purchasing experience.

Sheffield's university bookshops

As has been mentioned already, Sheffield has two bookshops

which specialize in university books. There is a fairly small
Bowes and Bowes shop (called A. B. Ward's at the time of the
survey) on the main site, where the Faculties of Arts, Social
Sciences, Architecture, Medicine, Pure Science and Law are
situated. The other shop, Hartley Seed's, is much bigger and
is both a general and university bookshop situated on the main
road close to the Faculties of Engineering and Materials
Technology. Hartley Seed's is opposite one of the hospitals
and thus is well situated for medical-book-selling, and it also
supplies books for the Sheffield Polytechnic bookshop which is
run by the Students' Union there.

The situation of Ward's bookshop at the university is not
very good for the passing general book trade, but, as there is
another Bowes and Bowes general bookshop in the city centre,
the university bookshop is much more limited to educational
book-selling than is the single, much larger, Hartley Seed's
shop. Whilst there is constant competition between the two
shops, there is a general understanding in the university that
the technologists are particularly catered for at Hartley Seed's
and that the arts people are particularly catered for at A. B.
Ward's. However, as Tables 7.1 and 7.2 show, neither shop
has a monopoly of any one faculty.

Table 7.1   Bookshops used (a)

Which bookshop do you normally buy your course books from?
Ward's; Hartley Seed's; Neither; Both
If neither, please say what shop, if any, you use

	All sample	1st year	2nd year	3rd year	4th year +
Ward's	49	45	53	51	45
Hartley Seed's	30	37	24	30	26
Both	14	14	14	12	24
Neither, other Sheffield	1	1	2	—	—
Neither, not Sheffield	3	2	5	3	3
None used	2	1	2	3	3
$n =$	760	265	221	236	38

Table 7.1 shows that 6 per cent of students do not use either Ward's or Hartley Seed's and that 14 per cent say they use both of them. Ward's is the shop used by the majority of all students, but the pattern of usage by year is confused, and not explicable except by a cyclical hypothesis of some loyalties switching from one shop to the other each year.

Table 7.2 gives a picture of differences between faculties and shows a preponderance of Arts, Social Sciences and Pure Science Faculties using Ward's, with Law, Engineering and Materials Technology clearly based on Hartley Seed's. Ward's has the edge on Hartley Seed's for medical students, but 28 per cent of these students, a fairly large proportion, say they use both shops. Architecture is the most divided faculty, with only a small majority for Ward's, but this faculty, as further data will show, comes very low in book-buying.

Table 7.2   Bookshops used (b)

	Arts	Soc. Sci.	Arch.	Law	Med.	P.Sci.	Eng.	Mat. Tech.
Ward's	67	55	45	20	47	64	11	26
Hartley Seed's	9	24	38	54	19	18	76	71
Both	9	17	17	17	28	12	10	3
Neither, other Sheffield	3	1	—	—	—	1	—	—
Neither, not Sheffield	10	3	—	4	4	1	1	—
None used	2	—	—	4	1	4	2	—
n =	129	121	29	46	78	225	101	31

Table 7.2 shows that, except in the Faculties of Arts and Materials Technology, 10 per cent at least of students shop at both bookshops, with medical students (who include both pre-clinicals and clinicals) by far the most numerous in using both shops. An interesting 10 per cent of arts students said they did not use either shop and bought their books outside Sheffield. In some cases these were students who said they had better bookshops in their home towns and did their purchasing there in vacations, and in a few cases (especially in modern

languages) students bought mainly by mail order from London because they considered they got better service.

One first-year electronics student whose home is in Birmingham wrote, 'Hudson's is superior in every way'. But a second-year mechanical engineer felt 'They are doing what they can. Sometimes even the biggest bookshops, like Foyle's in London, can't meet the public demand'.

Comments about the shops themselves usually showed understanding, and students seemed particularly to appreciate the difficulties of running bookshops on premises adapted from smaller shops which has resulted, especially in the case of Ward's, in a shop made up of several small rooms linked up to try to provide one shop. Whilst Hartley Seed's has three main parts and a basement, it is a reasonably sized shop and the sections do not seem too different from one another. Ward's is very much smaller and is made up of four small rooms plus a back room: this cannot be redesigned to produce a feeling of spaciousness, no matter how hard the owners try.

Student comments on the importance of space for university book-selling are quite interesting.

'Ward's is small and does not allow much space to have a good look round in your own time.' (2nd-year law)

'Ward's seem to be short of room. I feel quite sure a more spacious shop would be a great asset.' (3rd-year French)

'Both bookshops could do with larger premises considering the stock they are expected to carry.' (1st-year economic history, politics and law)

'The service is not so much at fault as the actual size of the shops. Conditions in both shops are rather cramped and not suitable to supply a university the size of Sheffield.' (1st-year town and regional planning)

One second-year mathematics student felt that Ward's could use its space better, though the shop has already been rearranged several times, with new fixtures, in recent years since it became a part of the Bowes and Bowes group. Some other comments reflected the problems of overcrowding, and sometimes students suggested services which would probably exacerbate the overcrowding. A third-year physics student wanted 'Some sort of catalogue of what they stock, even if they are sold out.' The classification of books on the shelves came in for adverse comment. An arts student felt that the books he wanted in music and history were 'all in a mess', and a third-year electrical engineer wanted better sub-classifications at Hartley Seed's because of the large number of books in his field. A social scientist felt that the classification of 'Pelicans' alphabetically by title was inferior to classification by author, and a third-year philosophy student had a problem in finding Sartre's *In Camera* which, he said, 'is in a collection of European plays and not under Sartre or under its title, so I had trouble finding it.'

In general, the student reaction at this stage seemed to be one of sympathy for the booksellers who were trying to do their jobs under difficult physical conditions. Some students clearly would like an index system, rather like the library catalogue, that would tell them where to find a book they wanted and, if it were not in stock, the current position about obtaining a copy.

Bookshop stocks

The problem of stock-holding in university bookshops is one of the most difficult in the book trade and at times, when one hears academic staff talking together, one gets an impression of shops run by idiots, stacked high with books that no one ever wants. It was, therefore, important to ask the under-graduates for their opinions on the stocks of the two university bookshops, and for this question pre-set response categories were used. The replies were given separately for each bookshop and so there are double tables for the years of study and for the faculties.

Table 7.3 shows that overall opinion on stock for the two bookshops is not favourable. At Ward's, 23 per cent of students consider the stock in their subject (or subjects) is good or very good, whilst 39 per cent think it is poor or very poor. At Hartley Seed's, 31 per cent consider the stock is good or very good, whilst 33 per cent consider it poor or very poor.

First-year students tend to be less critical than second- or third-year students, and this is especially the case at Hartley Seed's, where 42 per cent of first-year students rate the stock

Table 7.3 Bookshop stocks (*a*)

Do you think the stock in your subject(s) of the two Sheffield shops is:
Ward's Very good; Good; So-so; Poor; Very poor; Don't know?
Hartley Seed's Very good; Good; So-so; Poor; Very poor; Don't know?

	All sample	1st year	2nd year	3rd year	4th year +
		Replies for Ward's			
Very good	2	2	1	1	8
Good	21	21	19	19	49
So-so	33	34	33	37	16
Poor	26	27	25	26	19
Very poor	16	14	20	16	8
Don't know	2	3	1	1	—
n =	738	259	216	226	37
Score (excluding 'don't know')	42	41	39	40	58
		Replies for Hartley Seed's			
Very good	4	6	3	3	6
Good	27	36	24	23	49
So-so	28	26	31	29	20
Poor	21	16	25	23	20
Very poor	12	9	14	15	3
Don't know	5	6	4	6	3
n =	718	251	208	224	35
Score (excluding 'don't know')	49	54	44	44	62

good or very good, and only 25 per cent poor or very poor.
Students in the fourth year and over (mainly medicals) give
good marks to both shops.

The analysis of opinions by faculty is given in Table 7.4, and
here it is interesting to link the opinions with the shops most
used by various types of students and to consider these opinions
against the background of what has already been written in

previous pages of this book about the way in which the various students use books for their studies.

Table 7.4   Bookshop stocks (*b*)

	Replies for Ward's							
	Arts	Soc. Sci.	Arch.	Law	Med.	P.Sci.	Eng.	Mat. Tech.
Very good	2	2	—	—	5	2	—	—
Good	12	18	17	29	40	25	16	7
So-so	29	42	41	48	26	38	23	14
Poor	31	22	28	19	17	20	39	46
Very poor	27	15	10	5	10	12	20	25
Don't know	—	2	3	—	1	2	2	7
$n =$	129	120	29	42	77	220	93	28
Score (excluding 'don't know')	33	43	42	51	53	46	34	26

There was a 3 per cent non-response overall for Ward's. This was slightly higher in the third year than in other years, and disproportionately great in the Faculties of Engineering and Materials Technology.

	Replies for Hartley Seed's							
	Arts	Soc. Sci.	Arch.	Law	Med.	P.Sci.	Eng.	Mat. Tech.
Very good	—	4	7	10	3	5	7	3
Good	5	26	14	55	38	23	52	55
So-so	22	32	36	26	27	29	27	34
Poor	33	19	29	5	22	25	8	7
Very poor	37	11	14	—	5	9	3	—
Don't know	3	7	—	5	5	9	3	—
$n =$	120	115	28	42	73	213	98	29
Score (excluding 'don't know')	28	49	43	69	53	47	61	63

There was a 6 per cent non-response overall for Hartley Seed's. This was evenly distributed amongst years, but disproportionately great in the Faculties of Law and Materials Technology.

Hartley Seed's bookshop was shown in Table 7.2 to cater for the majority of students in Engineering (76 per cent), Materials Technology (71 per cent) and Law (54 per cent). For these three faculties, Hartley Seed's has good responses on opinions about its stock, with scores of 61, 63 and 69 respectively, which indicate more satisfaction than dissatisfaction. Ward's caters only for a minority of these students and, perhaps not surprisingly, gets only scores of 34, 26 and 51.

On the other hand, the majority of students in Arts (67 per cent), Pure Science (64 per cent) and Social Sciences (55 per cent) go to Ward's for their books. For these three faculties Ward's gets satisfaction scores of 33, 46 and 43. For the same faculties the scores for Hartley Seed's are 28, 47 and 49. The inference from these results is that arts students are very hard people to please, whilst the minority—pure science and social science students—who use Hartley Seed's are just marginally more satisfied than the majority who use Ward's.

The Faculty of Medicine has 47 per cent of students mainly using Ward's, 19 per cent at Hartley Seed's and 28 per cent who use both shops, and so it provides an interesting group with the greatest dual allegiance, and the satisfaction score is identical at 53 for both shops.

Architecture students are very divided, with only a small majority favouring Ward's (45 per cent) over Hartley Seed's (38 per cent), and 17 per cent using both. Their satisfaction scores of 42 for Ward's and 43 for Hartley Seed's are very similar.

Perhaps the most interesting conclusion to draw from these tables is not so much the differences of views about bookshop stocks as they relate to the two shops as the general differences between the faculties themselves. If we take the higher satisfaction score for each faculty, ignoring the bookshop at which it is given, we find the greatest satisfaction shown by the Faculties of Law (69), Materials Technology (63) and Engineering (61). Then come Medicine (53), Social Sciences (49), Pure Science (47), Architecture (43), and lastly Arts at 33. The three faculties where satisfaction is relatively high are also the faculties in which the highest satisfaction was shown in the guidance received from lecturers about the books students should buy (see Tables 5.14 and 5.16). This would seem to indicate that communications about the purchase of books are reasonably good in these three faculties, and it is indicative of more certainty on the part of staff (and thus of students and bookshops) about the books which undergraduates should obtain for themselves. There is less certainty in the other faculties, and the one faculty in which the certainty is clearly at its lowest point is the Arts Faculty. Since Ward's bookshop is the prime supplier of books to this faculty, it is not surprising that the satisfaction rating for this shop is lower than that at Hartley Seed's, even allowing for actual differences in the skills of the booksellers at the two shops. Any university bookshop catering for arts subjects must expect criticism from students— even though this dissatisfaction may have its ultimate cause in a lack of specific recommendations made by the lecturers to the booksellers.

Inadequate stocks were not seen solely as the bookseller's fault, and many students in their comments recognized that booksellers could not order books without receiving guidance from the lecturers. Amongst the many comments made by the students, only a small number can be given here, but pride of place must go to a third-year student of genetics and micro-biology who had clearly analysed the problem carefully and put forward the correct remedy:

'If lecturers were to inform the bookshops of what books
they intend to recommend and of how many students
were going to buy them, the bookshops could have them
in stock, in time, in adequate supply.'

How very right this student is and how very big is his 'if'. But as a rather more realistic third-year student of politics and history commented, 'The trouble is, if lecturers don't tell us what to get they're not likely to tell Ward's'.

Another student, this time a first-year English student, saw that staff-bookshop communications were not right:

'There is a need for closer liaison between the bookshops
and the University re course books, likely demands etc.
Last term the two parties spent most of their time
blaming each other for an inadequacy of certain essential
books.'

A third-year student reading Russian was more definite in his feelings about where the blame should be:

'The university bookshops are not given a comprehensive booklist in my subject. Therefore it is impossible to get books for weeks after the beginning of term. Could this be rectified?'

But students of French complained of inadequate stocking on the part of the bookseller:

'They tend to understock, so if you wait much more than a week before buying a book it's usually out of stock. If possible they should be persuaded to stock more actual course books.'

The importance of bookshops knowing well in advance about books was highlighted by a first-year town and regional planning student:

'When trying to purchase an architecture book at Hartley Seed's which was on the reading list it was discovered that the shop had not been given notice of the list. Consequently books were not in stock and there were 60 people on the course who could be wanting books.'

Students did not see any problem in bookshops holding large unsold stocks. As a second-year medical student explained:

'It would not harm them to stock all the popular and well used books in great quantities; they could sell them the year after if they were in excess.'

A second-year French student believed that

'If students found that shops tended to stock the correct number of books they would buy there instead of ordering elsewhere.'

But a second-year student of history and politics was less sure: 'There should be a better response to booklists presented by departments (or perhaps better booklists from departments, because booksellers say they don't sell out of books ordered by departments).'

The correct stocking of books in a university bookshop calls for enormous skills and the ability to decide, often on the flimsiest of evidence, how many copies of a book will *really* be wanted for the coming academic year. Booksellers keep careful records of their sales of the many titles they stock, and it would probably be a salutary experience for many lecturers to see just how few copies of supposedly essential books are actually sold by the university booksellers each year. When lecturers give incorrect advice the bookseller is placed in a hopeless position. A first-year law student wrote:

'Why can't the University give correct advice on books needed, as this year we were recommended a different contract casebook from the ones the shops were advised to stock.'

Fortunately major upsets such as these are not happening all the time, but it is not surprising that a first-year arts student wrote: 'In many cases the trouble is the delay in departments handing in lists and then getting the bookshops to believe them.'

Given that students are frequently disappointed when basic course books are not in stock at the local bookshop, it does seem a little strange to find complaints from them about too many books on the shelves which seem to be irrelevant to their needs. One third-year geographer put it thus:

'They seem to persist in buying books not recommended on the course at the expense of more relevant books, despite advice from departments.'

And a third-year dual geography/sociology student wrote:

'Too much concentration on fashionable books, e.g. trendy left-wing authors, especially in Sociology. They would do well to discover what books are required for the courses.'

Complaints about stocking of books which students felt were irrelevant to their interests came from chemistry, accountancy, politics, and law. But opinion was divided on this issue, and whilst those geography students quoted above were critical of breadth of stock, other geography students applauded a greater range:

'A wider variety of books in one subject should be available, preferably at a reasonable price.' (3rd-year geography)

'One or two copies of books which are not specially recommended for purchase but which are of interest to the subject would be useful.' (3rd-year geography)

In general the main theme running through all the comments about bookshop stocks emphasized the need for greater co-operation between the university lecturers and the bookshops, so that adequate titles in adequate numbers could be in stock for the beginning of the session when students wanted them and were prepared to buy them. It was recognized that there were faults on both sides and probably the timidity of the bookshops in understocking came in for most criticism, since few students saw any problem in holding unsold stock for sale twelve months later. In one or two cases students advocated a bookshop run by the university itself which, as a second-year politics student suggested, 'could deal more efficiently with ordering'. But this student did not explain why or how a university-run shop would be more efficient than one run by actual booksellers.

Perhaps the most revealing comment of all came from a third-year geology student who wrote, 'I am told that the stock of Geology books in both bookshops is abyssmal [*sic*].' He had not bought any books himself during the year.

Ordering books not in stock

With a quarter of a million titles in print and over thirty thousand new titles being published every year, no customer can expect every bookshop to have in stock every possible title. On the other hand, university undergraduates who have very limited book-needs not unnaturally expect that specialist bookshops whose whole *raison d'être* is to cater for their needs will have in stock the bulk of the books recommended for their courses. Students assume, not always correctly, that the bookshops have been informed, well in advance of the term's beginning, of those books which lecturers will require or expect their students to buy. If this has been done, then it is the booksellers' task to see that an adequate number of copies are in stock for would-be purchasers.

But no system is perfect, and students do realize that no bookseller will stock 100 copies of a book which is merely 'recommended' to a class of 100 students. So undergraduates are not always surprised when they find that a book which has been stocked in relatively small numbers has sold better than was expected and is now temporarily out of stock. There are also, of course, books temporarily out of print at the publishers, and dock strikes both at home and abroad can play havoc with deliveries of books. Taking all these matters into account, it would be surprising if an undergraduate did *not* have to order a book from time to time. When asked about ordering of books, 37 per cent of all the respondents said they had never ordered a book from their main bookshop.

Table 7.5   Ordering of books (*a*)

At the shop you ticked in Question 1, have you ever ordered a book not in stock?   Yes; No

If yes (*a*) about how many books altogether have you ordered?
    … books

	All sample	1st year	2nd year	3rd year	4th year +
No, not ordered	37	40	39	33	35
Yes, under 5	48	48	48	48	57
Yes, 5 to 9	10	10	8	13	5
Yes, 10 to 14	2	1	3	4	3
Yes, 15 to 19	1	—	2	1	—
Yes, 20 or more	1	1	1	1	—
n =	745	260	217	231	37

Table 7.5 might be expected to show that, as students progress from their first year through to their final year, their experience of ordering books increases. Although there is such a trend, Table 7.5 shows that it is a very slight one and by the third year 33 per cent of all students still have never ordered a book, and only 19 per cent have ordered five or more books in their whole university career of nearly three academic years.

Differences between faculties are much greater than differences between years, as Table 7.6 shows.

In this table the Arts Faculty stands out clearly from the rest, with only 22 per cent of students who have never ordered a book and 26 per cent who have ordered five or more. Whilst it is not surprising to find that 40 per cent or more of students in Engineering, Architecture, Materials Technology and Pure

Table 7.6   Ordering of books (b)

	Arts	Soc. Sci.	Arch.	Law	Med.	P.Sci.	Eng.	Mat. Tech.
No, none ordered	22	39	45	29	31	41	50	42
Yes, under 5	52	43	41	53	58	50	42	45
Yes, 5 to 9	17	13	14	18	6	7	5	3
Yes, 10 to 14	2	4	—	—	4	1	2	6
Yes, 15 to 19	3	1	—	—	—	—	—	3
Yes, 20 or more	4	—	—	—	—	—	1	—
$n =$	126	117	29	45	77	220	100	31

Science have never ordered books, the 39 per cent of social scientists who have never ordered books is unexpectedly high.

Those students who had experience of ordering books were asked if, in general, they thought that deliveries were fast or slow. Since the book trade spends a great deal of time on discussions about the slow delivery of books, it was felt that the opinions of the students might well be interesting. Generally speaking the opinion was that deliveries were slow rather than

Table 7.7   Speed of book deliveries (a)

(For those who had ordered books not in stock)
(b)   In general was delivery:
Very quick; Fairly quick; So-so; Fairly slow; Very slow?

	All sample	1st year	2nd year	3rd year	4th year+
Very quick	2	3	5	1	—
Fairly quick	28	30	22	27	42
So-so	24	19	25	27	21
Fairly slow	26	23	27	28	25
Very slow	20	25	21	16	13
n for above =	456	148	131	153	24
Score	42	41	40	48	48

M

quick, but 30 per cent of all students felt they were very quick or fairly quick and only 20 per cent thought they were very slow. The overall score of 42 on this question should not give publishers or booksellers much cause for congratulating themselves, but it might well have been lower.

Table 7.7 shows that opinions on the speed of deliveries were better amongst students in their third year or beyond, compared with those of the first- and second-year students.

Opinions varied more between faculties than between years, and Table 7.8 below shows how satisfaction was at its lowest among the arts students. Engineering, Pure Science and Law were the most satisfied, and Architecture, Materials Technology, Social Sciences and Medicine were fairly similar in their scores, lying between the two extremes.

Table 7.8   Speed of book deliveries (*b*)

	Arts	Soc. Sci.	Arch.	Law	Med.	P.Sci.	Eng.	Mat. Tech.
Very quick	3	1	—	3	—	5	—	—
Fairly quick	15	25	19	34	29	33	39	29
So-so	24	23	31	31	14	19	39	24
Fairly slow	27	32	44	16	35	23	12	24
Very slow	31	18	6	16	22	20	10	24
n for above =	95	71	16	32	51	125	49	17
Score	33	39	41	48	38	49	52	40

It should be remembered, though, that the views analysed in Tables 7.7 and 7.8 are purely individual and subjective, and what one person may consider fairly quick another person may consider to be very slow. It was very difficult to devise a form of question that would elicit objective evidence about times taken over book deliveries, and finally it was decided that a question about the *fastest* delivery might be most useful. (As I am still awaiting a book ordered nearly two years ago from one of the shops, a question on *slowest* deliveries did not seem to be of much value.) So those students who *had* ordered books not in stock were asked, 'Can you give a time for your fastest delivery?' and the analysis categories were decided after the replies had been examined.

Table 7.9 shows that the modal category for the *fastest* delivery was between two and three weeks, a category particularly favoured by students in the third year of study or above who, in Table 7.7, had shown themselves to consider deliveries in general to be more speedy than did students in the first or second year. It does not seem unreasonable, therefore, to conclude that, if a student can obtain a book on order in under three weeks, he will be reasonably satisfied. This may seem completely out of line with some book-trade discussions which talk about days—and even express some hoped-for deliveries in terms of hours, albeit that it is in large multiples of hours—but perhaps the students are more realistic than some booksellers about book orders and deliveries.

Table 7.9 Speed of delivery (*a*)

(For those who had ordered books not in stock)
(*c*) Can you give a time for your fastest delivery? ...

	All sample	1st year	2nd year	3rd year	4th year+
Under 4 days	3	7	2	1	—
5 days, under a week	6	9	6	3	—
1 week, but under 2	24	20	26	25	36
2 weeks, but under 3	28	22	26	37	36
3 weeks, but under 4	21	22	21	20	14
4 weeks or over	18	20	19	15	14
n for above =	325	104	98	109	14

Times quoted for fastest deliveries varied greatly between students, but the faculty differences shown in Table 7.10 would seem to indicate that Law and Engineering do slightly better than the other faculties, and that Medicine and Social Sciences have the longest waits.

The student respondents were asked if they could give the names of any books ordered for which they had had a long wait. Response to this question was limited, since 37 per cent of

Table 7.10   Speed of delivery (*b*)

	Arts	Soc. Sci.	Arch.	Law	Med.	P.Sci.	Eng.	Mat. Tech.
Under 4 days	1	3	—	4	—	6	3	—
5 days, under a week	7	3	10	8	—	6	6	9
1 week, but under 2	26	23	20	28	21	20	32	27
2 weeks, but under 3	26	22	30	36	32	26	38	36
3 weeks, but under 4	19	30	20	16	26	21	18	—
4 weeks or over	21	18	20	8	21	21	3	27
n for above $=$	70	60	10	25	34	81	34	11

respondents had said that they had never ordered a book at all and a further 34 per cent, who had claimed to have ordered books, did not cite any titles in reply to this question. In all 209 students out of the sample of 763 did cite books ordered for which they had had a long wait. Of these 209, 179 cited one book, 27 cited two books and three cited three books. Of the 243 books cited, 63 were cited by arts students, 44 by social scientists, 7 by architects, 17 by law students, 31 by medicals, 62 by pure scientists, 10 by engineers and 8 by materials technologists.

Comments on problems of delivery were few. One law student did feel that a three weeks' wait was too long and that there should be a faster delivery. A second-year French student felt it was both quicker and cheaper to obtain his books by post from Grant and Cutler in London. A student in the first-year integrated biology course wrote:

'It's no use having to wait half way through the year until you can get a book. By that time you may not need the book any more and you've wasted your money.'

And a disillusioned third-year economist wrote of bookshop assistants:

'Tell them not to give false impressions over delivery dates. When you order a book they always tell you that it will only take about a fortnight, but it never does.'

A first-year medical student felt that books on order sometimes stood too long in the bookshop:

'When an ordered book arrives you are not always notified. Infuriating, since you will not buy elsewhere if you think it is on order. More careful checks should be made.'

A third-year geography student claimed that at one bookshop the staff had refused to order a paperback copy of a book for him because they had a hardback copy in stock. If this was true then clearly the assistant was very much at fault.

The bookshop staff

One of the greatest problems in bookselling, as in most retail businesses, is that the customer comes most into contact with the least qualified and least experienced staff—the ordinary assistants. Such are the wages and prospects in British bookselling that it is not easy to attract and retain good staff, and in *university* bookshops especially knowledgeable staff are

Table 7.11 Helpfulness of bookshop staff (*a*)

At the shop ticked in Question 3.1, do you find the staff:
Very helpful; Fairly helpful; So-so; Fairly unhelpful; Very unhelpful?

| | *Replies for Ward's* | | | | |
	All sample	1st year	2nd year	3rd year	4th year +
Very helpful	18	19	17	18	24
Fairly helpful	43	43	38	48	53
So-so	27	25	29	28	18
Fairly unhelpful	9	11	14	4	—
Very unhelpful	2	2	3	3	6
n for above =	368	118	114	119	17
Score	66	67	64	69	73

(*Table 7.11 continued*)

| | Replies for Hartley Seed's | | | | |
	All sample	1st year	2nd year	3rd year	4th year +
Very helpful	18	21	10	21	10
Fairly helpful	53	54	56	48	60
So-so	23	18	27	25	30
Fairly unhelpful	6	6	8	6	—
Very unhelpful	—	1	—	—	—
n for above =	228	95	52	71	10
Score	71	72	68	71	70

essential. It cannot be expected that undergraduates will make demands upon booksellers equal to those of the academic staff, but it is important that young student book-buyers be treated reasonably by bookshop assistants. When asked about the helpfulness of the staff at the two Sheffield shops, most students gave them good marks. Again, the question was related to the bookshop most used, and so there are two sets of tables for both the years and the faculties.

As Table 7.11 shows, 61 per cent of all students felt that Ward's staff were fairly or very helpful and 71 per cent felt this for Hartley Seed's staff. Only 11 per cent and 6 per cent respectively felt the staff were unhelpful at all.

In Table 7.11 there are no discernible patterns of opinion between students in different years, though satisfaction does seem to be at a low ebb in the second year. Differences between faculties, however, were, not unexpectedly, much greater and these are shown in Table 7.12.

The architecture students, who, by faculty, are the lowest spenders on books, also give the lowest rating for helpfulness of assistants at the two bookshops, but as there is so little trade in architecture books this figure is best put to one side. For the rest it is interesting to see that the arts students, as usual, are less satisfied than most other faculties, but, perhaps surprisingly with their reputation for protest, the social scientists are reasonably satisfied at both shops. The minority groups of engineers and materials technologists who use Ward's rather than Hartley Seed's are among the least satisfied students.

Table 7.12   Helpfulness of bookshop staff (*b*)

Replies for Ward's

	Arts	Soc. Sci.	Arch.	Law	Med.	P.Sci.	Eng.	Mat. Tech.
Very helpful	10	27	25	—	14	20	27	13
Fairly helpful	40	36	8	78	62	46	36	38
So-so	34	29	33	11	16	25	9	50
Fairly unhelpful	13	6	33	—	5	8	18	—
Very unhelpful	2	2	—	11	3	2	9	—
n for above =	87	66	12	9	37	138	11	8
Score	60	70	56	64	70	69	61	67

Replies for Hartley Seed's

	Arts	Soc. Sci.	Arch.	Law	Med.	P.Sci.	Eng.	Mat. Tech.
Very helpful	8	14	18	17	20	23	20	14
Fairly helpful	58	59	9	50	53	58	48	73
So-so	25	17	36	25	20	18	31	5
Fairly unhelpful	8	10	27	8	7	3	1	9
Very unhelpful	—	—	9	—	—	—	—	—
n for above =	12	29	11	24	15	40	75	22
Score	66	69	50	69	72	76	72	74

There were hardly any adverse comments written in by students, though one first-year arts student did ask for improved civility from 'certain members' of Ward's, and a third-year law student said he would like 'a little more friendliness' at both bookshops.

A more specialized comment came from a second-year philosophy and politics student. He wanted 'particular people in the shops who are responsible for particular areas of study and who are available for queries or suggestions'. This point was made more explicitly by a second-year English student who wrote that 'It would help if there was at least one assistant whose speciality was English Literature.' The problem is, of course, that, in bookshops with limited staff, any range of specialism covered by the staff is bound to remain quite broad, and no assistant can hope to match the specialized knowledge of a diligent student.

The purchase of books

As has been shown on previous pages, the need for books varies considerably between the many courses of study pursued in the university, and university students cannot be considered as a homogeneous group in so far as their book-needs are concerned. It could not be expected, therefore, that student expenditure on books would be uniform between years and faculties, especially since previous studies already referred to have established that differences do occur.

The Sheffield survey was carried out near to the end of the Lent Term of 1972, and it seemed reasonable to suppose that most students had purchased the books they needed by then.

It is not claimed from this survey that all the sums of money quoted by the student respondents are accurate to the nearest ten pence, or that some students may not have overstated their expenditure because they felt some small shame about their meagre spending. But in reading through the questionnaires I got a strong feeling that most students were being honest about their spending on books—at times disarmingly honest—and the fact that 4 per cent of all students simply reported that they had spent nothing on books over the past academic year does lend support to my belief that there was little over-reporting of expenditure.

Tables 7.13 and 7.14 give frequency distributions of the years and the faculties, with average expenditure entered for each category.

Table 7.13 shows the expected decline in spending from an initial £20.84 average in the first year, through £16.84 in the second year, down to £11.48 in the third year. The sum of £20.56 for the fourth year and beyond is almost wholly due to medical students, who are relatively big spenders on books. The first-to-third-year columns show how no students in the first year claimed to have spent less than £3 on books, but by the third year 18 per cent of students were in this category.

Table 7.13   Expenditure on books (*a*)

About how much money do you reckon you have spent on books for study this session (i.e. 1971–2 academic year)?   £

£	All sample	1st year	2nd year	3rd year	4th year +
None	4	—	3	8	5
Under 3	4	—	4	10	—
3–5	11	4	9	21	—
6–8	8	5	11	9	3
9–11	12	9	11	16	18
12–14	7	8	8	6	3
15–17	13	16	14	8	13
18–20	14	19	14	8	18
21–23	2	4	1	1	5
24–29	11	13	11	8	11
30–35	9	13	9	4	16
36 or over	6	8	6	2	8
n =	741	260	218	225	38
Average expenditure in £	16.80	20.84	16.84	11.48	20.56

It can also be seen in the columns that spending on books varies greatly amongst students and that there is not a 'normal distribution' in any column.

The complexity of the situation is illustrated when we turn to the analysis by faculties in Table 7.14.

As Table 7.14 shows, the variation between faculties is quite considerable, ranging from £9.96 in Architecture to £22.43 in Law. Table 7.15 gives the faculties in order of expenditure, and the scores for guidance from lecturers on what to buy.

As Table 7.15 shows, the Law Faculty stands out as being the one with the highest average expenditure on books and the highest satisfaction rating for advice from lecturers on what to buy. But after Law the two columns do not keep a clear correlation between spending and advice. Medical students and arts students come second and third in spending, but are not

so well satisfied about lecturers' advice on book-buying as are students in Materials Technology, Engineering or Architecture.
Materials technology students come higher than social

Table 7.14 Expenditure on books (*b*)

£	Arts	Soc. Sci.	Arch.	Law	Med.	P.Sci.	Eng.	Mat. Tech.
None	2	1	4	—	4	6	5	3
Under 3	2	3	—	—	1	7	8	—
3–5	7	5	36	—	4	14	17	9
6–8	7	10	14	2	1	11	4	9
9–11	8	18	14	2	11	12	17	6
12–14	9	12	7	4	3	6	6	6
15–17	13	13	18	22	13	11	11	13
18–20	12	14	4	20	20	14	15	13
21–23	5	1	—	7	1	1	2	—
24–29	11	9	—	30	13	5	9	28
30–35	8	9	4	11	24	8	4	13
36 and over	14	5	—	2	8	5	1	—
n =	122	120	28	46	75	219	99	32
Average expenditure in £	19.42	16.88	9.96	22.43	21.26	14.24	13.09	18.84

Table 7.15 Faculties in order of expenditure compared with lecturers' guidance

	Average expenditure (£)	Score for buying-advice
Law	22.43	75
Medicine	21.26	61
Arts	19.42	54
Materials Technology	18.84	70
Social Science	16.88	52
Pure Science	14.24	60
Engineering	13.09	64
Architecture	9.96	64

scientists in average expenditure and have a much higher appreciation rating for advice, seventy compared to fifty-two (which is the lowest of all). Pure scientists and engineers are quite close in spending and rating for advice, whilst architecture students have the lowest average expenditure of all, but have a higher advice rating than four other faculties.

The explanation for these variations cannot be simple, but taking together all the known factors about the various faculties, the following tentative explanation is offered.

The law students *need* books for their studies, as they use books in the way that scientists use laboratory equipment. The Law Faculty is a one-department faculty with very little in the way of courses shared with other departments. Contact between staff and students is close, and advice about books is generally consistent and specific. If a textbook on a particular aspect of law is *needed* both staff and students see the sense of this.

In Medicine the students are in some ways similar to the law students, but the Faculty is much larger, covers both medicine and dentistry, and has many departments at pre-clinical and clinical level. Students see that they *need* books for constant reference but co-ordination of guidance on buying is difficult, especially at the clinical level, where many teachers are consultants and only hold part-time or honorary lectureships. Thus guidance to students is difficult with such a range of study to be covered.

The Arts Faculty contained some of the highest spenders on books, with some students claiming to have spent over £60 in the year on books alone. Once again this is a faculty in which many students recognize that personal ownership of set texts is almost unavoidable because these (rather as in Law) are the basic tools of the year's study. But the Arts Faculty is far from homogeneous in its forms of subject and twenty-five subjects can be studied in the first year with fifteen single schools and sixty-nine other schools to follow in the second and third years. With this great diversity, one must appreciate the differences between the foreign-language degrees, where buying and guidance both seem more systematic, and subjects such as philosophy or history where guidance is much less clearly defined.

The Materials Technology Faculty is a fairly small faculty, in some ways like Law, though it is not one department or so much dependent as is Law upon books as the basis for study.

Nevertheless, the impression was gained of a faculty where guidance was, generally speaking, better than in the other technology and science departments.

Expenditure on books in the Social Sciences Faculty was not particularly high for a faculty where books form so large a part of the curriculum. In this faculty it was clear that a great amount of reading was expected of students, but as many of the students used books only for chapter references and in some subjects (such as sociology) very few actual textbooks were recommended, the actual spending on books was not very high.

The Pure Science and Engineering Faculties' average expenditure of £14.24 and £13.09 respectively placed them low on the list, but in both these faculties students commented on the lack of a felt need for books in certain courses. This appeared to be particularly the case in courses such as mathematics, though it was not so in the biological science departments which are in the Pure Science Faculty.

The architecture students had the lowest average expenditure of all faculties, though their rating on lecturers' guidance about buying came joint third. Here again there seemed to be little need of *books* in many of their courses, though reports, pamphlets and such publications are in constant use.

It must be borne in mind, therefore, that book-needs do vary very greatly between different types of courses, and that a low average expenditure by students may be coupled with quite high satisfaction about lecturers' guidance on book-buying if the actual numbers of perceived book-needs are low. If a student really does feel that all he needs to buy for this year's course is three basic text books at £4 each, then an expenditure of £12 could be quite satisfactory to him and his lecturers.

Prices of books

The price of books does, naturally, play quite an important part in the apportionment of students' money for books, and so a question about prices was asked of them. It was very difficult to know how best to approach this topic and, in the end, I decided to ask a *general* question about opinions on book prices and then to ask students to give actual *examples* of books which they considered to be expensive. Tables 7.16 and 7.17 give the results for the general question.

Table 7.16   Prices of books (a)

Allowing for differences between hard-cover and paperback editions, do you think *in general* that the prices of books in your subject(s) are: Very high; Fairly high; So-so; Fairly low; Very low?

	All sample	1st year	2nd year	3rd year	4th year +
Very high	27	25	27	29	42
Fairly high	49	49	47	51	37
So-so	19	22	18	15	21
Fairly low	5	4	6	6	—
Very low	—	—	1	—	—
n =	754	263	219	234	38
Score	75	74	73	76	80

As Table 7.16 shows, a score of 75 indicates that book prices were, on the whole, felt to be fairly high. This will not come as any surprise to booksellers in this country, who have argued for many years that the holding down of book prices after the Second World War conditioned people to false ideas of what books should cost and that recent increases have only been dragging buyers, albeit reluctantly, into the harsher realities of higher prices long ago recognized and accepted by people on the Continent and in the USA. Views on prices do not vary much from year to year between the first- and third-years, and in the fourth year and above medical students, as always, affect the score. This can be better seen in the analysis by faculties in Table 7.17.

In Table 7.17 the score ranges from Arts at 64 to Law at 81. The fact that the Faculties of Law and Medicine, the two highest spenders on books, also agree that book prices are high adds weight to the point that in these two faculties the students recognize that they *must* purchase books, no matter how highly priced some of them may be. A similar situation seems to occur

Table 7.17   Prices of books (*b*)

	Arts	Soc. Sci.	Arch.	Law	Med.	P.Sci.	Eng.	Mat. Tech.
Very high	17	24	28	36	38	33	22	22
Fairly high	37	50	48	53	47	48	52	69
So-so	31	21	21	11	14	12	24	9
Fairly low	13	5	—	—	—	6	2	—
Very low	1	—	3	—	—	—	—	—
$n =$	127	119	29	45	78	223	101	32
Score	64	73	75	81	80	77	74	78

in Materials Technology, where buying is commonplace and prices are regarded as high. The most interesting faculty is Arts, where a surprising 14 per cent of students actually felt that the price of books was low. This is a clear reflection of the differences of book usage between arts and science students. Even with paperback editions, science and technology books full of diagrams, formulae and illustrations cannot but be expensive to produce for a restricted market. But if one can purchase paperback copies of English classics or popular 'Pelican' books on the social issues of the day as one's university books, then book prices need not appear to be too high. I have no specific data from the survey on this point, but I would hazard a guess that whereas many law, medical, science and technology students may, albeit reluctantly, be prepared to spend £6 or £7 on one book, very few students in Arts or Social Sciences do so.

Student comments on book prices were surprisingly few, and those which were made tended to deal in economic matters such as discounts or net prices. A second-year accountancy student who had spent £30 on books during the year wrote, 'Abolish retail price maintenance on books' and a first-year student of economics and business studies wanted to 'Reduce monopoly pricing tendencies by reducing the demand for their books'.

Two other students were annoyed by the current practice of increasing book prices by putting small adhesive discs with new higher prices over the original prices on the dust-jackets. A second-year geology student wrote, 'Do not charge "new" higher prices for books that are already in stock by covering up old prices with a sticker.'

In most cases these stickers are affixed by publishers and have nothing to do with booksellers, who are embarrassed by them. But to the buyer all copies of books look alike and so a second-year English student who had spent £50 on books wrote: '*Beowulf*, edited by C. L. Wren, was seen in Ward's on Thursday marked 26/-. On the following Saturday morning this was covered over with a £1.50 sticker. Tell Ward's to sell the books they have bought at the original price'.

The question asking students to give actual examples of books which they had bought which they considered to be very expensive produced the response shown in Table 7.18.

Table 7.18   Expensive books

Can you give any examples of books you have bought which you consider to be very expensive?

%	No. of students	Books cited
30	228	no answer
45	345	1
14	106	2
2	19	3
0·4	3	4
$n =$	473	624
4	32	publisher or series cited
4	30	general comment on expensiveness

The actual examples cited by the students demonstrated a number of interesting attitudes to book prices. Not unnaturally there was a number of books which appeared to be cited simply because they were expensive, no matter what their value or size might be. Examples of these were:

Conybeare, *Textbook of Medicine*, £8 (4th-year medicine)

Woodworth and Schlosberg, *Experimental Psychology*, said to be 'over £9' by a second-year psychologist who had *not* bought it

Gray's *Anatomy*, £8 (several medical students), and Last's *Anatomy*, also £8

Timoshenko and Young, *Strength of Materials*, £8 (3rd-year mechanical engineering)

Shrock and Twenhofel, *Principles of Invertebrate Paleontology*, £7.45 (several geologists)

The most expensive single book, cited by a student of law, was Whiteman and Wheatcroft, *Income Tax and Surtax*, which was said to be 'about £13'.

In the naming of books such as those given above it was clear that any book priced at about £8 in 1972 could be considered intrinsically expensive, irrespective of merit or value for study. The one book singled out for more citation than any others was Lehninger's *Biochemistry* at £8.50, which had apparently been given as an essential text for a large number of students on the integrated biology course. At this price the one book accounted for nearly half the year's expenditure on books of several students but, as the lecturer who recommended it had stressed its importance, one of the bookshops that year sold over a hundred copies.

Other books at or below £5 were named by some students, and usually these were textbooks in science or technology. Examples are:

Batchelor, *Fluid Dynamics*, £4 (3rd-year mathematics)

Banister Fletcher, *History of Architecture*, £4.70 (several architects)

Levitt, *Introduction to Plant Physiology*, £5 (3rd-year botany)

Ollier, *Weathering*, £4.50 (3rd-year geography/geology)

Flett, *Mathematical Analysis*, £4.50 (3rd-year mathematics)

Many students did not say specifically whether they were quoting hardback or paperback editions in their examples, but some did make the point that even in *paperback* editions they considered some books to be expensive. Examples of these are:

Peterssen, *Meteorology*, £3.50 (1st-year geography)

Street on *Torts*, £2.50 (1st-year law)

Lewis and Reinhold, *Roman Civilization*, £1.85 (1st-year pre-history and archaeology)

Smith, *Circuits Devices and Systems*, £4.20 (1st-year electrical engineering)

Billmeyer, *Textbook of Polymer Science*, £4.30 (1st-year materials technology)

Some comments on hardback and paperback editions showed that students were not unaware of the general costliness of case-bound editions and the relative cheapness of the student or paperback editions. But, even so, students often felt that to pay nearly £5 for a paperback edition seemed very high.

One first-year law student wrote:

'In general, to pay £2.50 for a paperback book, although comparatively probably cheap, is still extortionate.'

A third-year student of Russian commented: 'The "Bradda" paperback editions of Russian books are extremely expensive.' And a second-year student of pre-history and archaeology considered 'In general paperbacks costing about £1 are the worst value, e.g. E. R. Wolf's *Peasants*.'

At this point the attitudes can be seen to be changing from consideration of price alone to that of 'value for money', and students were by no means unaware of the problems of academic publishing—though they were not always too sympathetic. A third-year metallurgy student said that most of his textbooks were rarely in paperback and therefore were expensive. A first-year electrical engineer noted that 'copies of electronics books must be new editions because of the change in approach to the subject', and he himself had spent £30 on books that year. A third-year sociologist wrote that 'American readers' were expensive. A slightly different view was that of a second-year mathematics student, who wrote that 'Most recommended books are too expensive and just a repeat of lecture notes.' His comment was unlike that of the first-year materials technologist who commented, 'The books purchased have proved to be pretty good value for money, although a couple were quite expensive.' This latter comment reflects favourably on the *faculty* first-year book-list issued for materials technologists.

But not all comments necessarily made such good sense. A third-year electrical engineer who had spent £10 on books that year wrote, 'I avoid the expensive ones even though I might need them.' But the prize must go to the third-year geologist who wrote, 'All my books are expensive, that's why I don't buy any': he had spent nothing on books that year.

A second-year English student wrote that 'I think our books are cheap compared with those used in science subjects', and generally speaking there were few adverse comments about high prices in themselves. What the arts students did complain of was books which seemed highly priced for what they were— such as *The Murder of Charles the Good* in Harper 'Torchbooks' at £1.30 (2nd-year history student) and Robbe Grillet's *La Jalousie* in Methuen '20th-Century Texts' at 88p for 'only 100 pages' (3rd-year combined arts). Foreign texts, biblical commentaries and sixteenth-century poetry were all types of books considered to be generally expensive.

Taken overall, the student comments on book prices seemed usually to be made more in sorrow than in anger. Two biblical studies students were unpleasantly surprised to have discovered that Bruce's *Hebrews* had risen from £1.75 to £3.50, but this was an exception. For the most part students did seem to recognize in a rough way that many academic books were likely to be expensive because of their limited market. Comments on high prices were by no means always linked to low personal spending, and many comments about prices came from students who had spent well above the average for their own faculty. The most striking comment in this vein was from a second-year English student who had spent £60 on books that year, but still felt that Robinson's *Complete Works of Chaucer* was expensive at £2.50. A few students felt that some books were expensive if they were only going to use them for one year, but even here there was no complete agreement; one student felt that the *Nouveau Petit Larousse* was expensive for a student studying French for only one year, but another first-year student wrote that although it was over £4 it was 'well worth it'.

There were no questions in the questionnaire which asked *directly* about buying or selling of second-hand books and, by hindsight, this can now be seen to have been an unfortunate omission. However, there were very few unsolicited comments from students about second-hand books and hardly anyone made the point that he saved a lot of money by buying second-hand. There were a few students here and there, in law and in science, who obviously bought new only when forced to do so, but for the most part students did not seem to engage on a large scale in second-hand trading and at both departmental and Union Bookshop (which sells only second-hand) level there did not seem to be any tremendous amount of activity for a university with 5,000 undergraduates.

Suggestions for improvements

In the last question in this section of the questionnaire all respondents were asked if they had any suggestions to offer for improving the service of the university bookshops. Forty-

Table 7.19 Improving bookshop service (a)

Please give any suggestions for improving the service of the university bookshops.

	All sample	1st year	2nd year	3rd year	4th year +
No answer	43	42	39	45	53
Better university/bookshop co-operation	34	34	32	37	24
Keep basic books in stock	30	29	34	23	53
Generally bigger stock of books	11	10	8	14	18
Improve shop layout/enlarge shop	10	9	10	11	6
Improve service of ordered books	6	10	3	6	—
Better informed bookshop staff	3	4	3	3	—
Set up university/union bookshop	3	3	5	1	—
Second-hand service wanted	2	1	3	1	—
More student editions of books	2	1	3	3	—
n (excluding 'no answer')=	498	168	164	149	17

three per cent of all students had no suggestions of any kind to offer and, as Table 7.19 shows, the second-year students were those with the greatest proportion (61 per cent) offering advice. By far the most comments dealt with better co-operation between the university departments and the bookshops and (clearly linked with this) the need for the shops to have the basic recommended books in stock at all times. Larger stocks of books, i.e. a greater *variety* of books, were not such an important factor as the *basic* books, and this is a point to which the University Bookshops Facilities Committee, working with bookshops, has subsequently given serious attention (see Appendix I).

As Table 7.19 shows, two types of comment stood out clearly from all the others, but, in considering the smaller categories, the 10 per cent comment on improving shop layouts and enlarging should be noted. Both shops have done their best to improve their layout over time but, as has been said previously, both of them, like Topsy, have 'just growed' and neither is in a purpose-built shop. As the Ward's shop is on a site owned by the University and is due for demolition, serious thought must be given to what happens when that shop is pulled down. Demands for a Union or university bookshop were quite low at 3 per cent and, generally speaking, there did seem to be some realization that the professionals who run the present bookshops do their best and that book-selling is perhaps best left to booksellers.

In the analysis of comments by faculty there were some interesting differences and, overall, the arts and social sciences had more comments to offer than the sciences and technology.

Suggestions for better co-operation between university and bookshops came especially from materials technologists, but they were also the lowest proportion (21 per cent) to comment about the need for basic books to be kept in stock, whereas 42 per cent of medical students were concerned about this. Not surprisingly, perhaps, architecture students had comments to offer on shop layout and premises generally. The humanities, and especially law, seemed less happy over deliveries of ordered books than did the sciences and technologies.

Individual comments made by students ranged from points of detail to complete condemnation of the profit motive. A few students obviously felt that some sort of catalogue would help

Table 7.20 Improving bookshop service (*b*)

	Arts	Soc. Sci.	Arch.	Law	Med.	P.Sci.	Eng.	Mat. Tech.
No answer	26	31	34	28	47	50	60	63
Better university/ bookshop co-operation	33	33	36	35	29	37	24	50
Keep basic books in stock	33	27	23	30	42	26	30	21
Generally bigger stock of books	9	9	—	8	13	13	19	—
Improve shop layout/enlarge shop	7	9	27	8	9	9	16	7
Improve service of ordered books	9	7	5	11	4	3	3	7
Better informed bookshop staff	3	3	9	5	—	3	3	—
Set up university/ union bookshop	3	6	—	3	—	3	—	7
Second-hand service wanted	1	4	—	—	—	3	—	—
More student editions of books	3	1	—	—	2	2	5	—
n (excluding 'no answer') =	116	99	22	37	45	128	37	14

them in the bookshops, especially at the beginning of the session. A fourth-year medical student wanted 'A list of recommended books displayed with each subject, indicating whether or not they are available and if not whether on order.' A first-year social scientist wanted to go even further and have bookshops issue lists, categorized under subject headings, of new books available, which would be sent to the halls of residence, libraries, Union and so on—in effect an accessions list such as the university library was issuing monthly at the time of the survey but which was later discontinued. A third-year engineer wanted more specialized bookshops for arts, medicine, science etc. 'à la Oxbridge', though he did not say what advantage this would bring.

A handful of students wanted the academic staff to set themselves up as amateur booksellers.

'The lecturers could buy course books in bulk to reduce prices.' (3rd-year mathematics and computing)

'Knock down the bookshops and obtain books through the department direct from the publishers.' (2nd-year Spanish)

The mathematician did not suggest where the capital was to be obtained for buying the books, and the Spanish student was clearly unaware of the Net Book Agreement which fixes book prices, and of the general disinclination of publishers to supply books direct to consumers and thus reduce practically every bookseller in the country to bankruptcy.

Support for a Union bookshop was not at all strong and a second-year geology student who advocated this clearly expected all books to be sold at wholesale prices, thus assuming that the shop would have no overheads to bear. A first-year chemical engineer was even critical of the current Union Bookshop for selling its second-hand stock at prices which he considered were too high.

A first-year law student had an interesting comment to make about stealing in bookshops. He wanted the shops to have more 'open-plan' layouts because 'though I am straight as a die, bookshops often give me the impression of being watched and this takes my mind off the books. I have personal friends who have been forced out of business through Eton boy-shoppers in Windsor and so I realize the staff have to be wary, but if a more open plan were used everyone would be happy except the light-fingered brigade.'

Certainly pilfering in bookshops is a source of serious loss to booksellers and it is interesting to note that the law student claims that such behaviour occurs at secondary level as well as at the higher level of education.

However, it should not be thought that all comments on bookshop service were adverse or dispiriting.

'I think the bookshops are offering quite good service.' (3rd-year chemical engineering)

'In general I have no difficulty in finding the books required for my course as co-ordination between bookshops and university seems good.' (3rd-year civil engineering)

'I find the service perfectly adequate. The faults and delays are caused by printers, binders etc.' (3rd-year biblical studies)

Such comments offer some balm to the hard-pressed bookseller who is trying to supply a reasonable service. Perhaps the last comment of all should be reserved for the second-year student of biochemistry who advocated, 'Start a non-profit-making bookshop.' He may rest assured that quite a number of people have already done so unintentionally and that, were he able to see the accounts of all the university bookshops now operating on a supposed profit-making basis in this country, he would probably find several in his advocated category.

Chapter 8

Conclusions

Introduction

The research described in the previous chapters of this book was derived from a theoretical model of a communication network between university lecturers, students, librarians and booksellers, but the emphasis throughout has been on the use of books by undergraduate students.

In the early stages of research in any aspect of any discipline, researchers are compelled to work with crude categories; indeed it can be argued that a great deal of research is concerned with the refining of categories of data even though the disciplines are as different as physics and sociology.

Certainly I have myself found in previous research into book-reading that greater understanding comes when one is able to differentiate between different sorts of books and thus different sorts of readers. In my two previous books on general reading I used a work-leisure model in which academic books were obviously at the 'work' end of the continuum. If we think in functional terms, it is sensible to ask questions about the reasons why people need books for the activity in which they are involved. There is a general assumption that university study does involve students in the use of books, but beyond this assumption there does not seem to have been sufficient consideration given to the *different* ways in which students pursuing different courses make use of books for study.

My main conclusions from this research into books and students are that, in general, students are able to pursue successfully courses of study for degrees with less use of books than might be expected.

From this general conclusion one should go on to consider *differences* between various types of students, especially in the courses they are following, and it is then possible to distinguish some disciplines in which books play a larger part than in others.

Having looked at the general and the particular aspects in

this way, it is reasonable to ask whether the situation which has been discovered is immutable or whether it is possible to say, without passing a subjective moral judgment, if things might be changed so as to enable people involved in the use of books in the university to improve their mode of operation to the greater satisfaction of all concerned.

On books in general

The theoretical diagram on page 5 demonstrated how complex is the network of communications possible between four groups of people. The university lecturers were singled out as the key people in the process, since they were the initiators in selecting books for undergraduate study. The most important line of communication is from the lecturer to the student who must be advised about reading. This advice requires the lecturer to advise students about reading priorities, about textbooks and set books, about those books which it may be desirable or even essential to purchase, and about borrowing from the library. To ensure that the advice is backed up by the *availability* of books recommended, the lecturer must inform and instruct both library and bookseller as to these needs, otherwise the students will be unable to carry out the advice given to them.

In courses where there are several lecturers co-operating in the teaching, and where students have clearly-determined courses to follow with very few options, departmental or even faculty reading-lists are feasible. But no matter how co-ordinated these guides may be, the ultimate decisions come from individual lecturers. I have been greatly impressed by general reading-lists issued by departments (such as Geography and Geology) or even faculties (such as Materials Technology) where it is clear that considerable thought and care have been given to publishing sensible and reasonable lists for students. That these do not always have the desired results is not always easily understandable. For example, all materials technology students receive faculty reading-lists in October, yet the survey showed that in the following February the bulk of students replied on the questionnaires that they received reading-lists from only few or none of their courses. This may have been a misunderstanding over 'faculty' lists and 'course' lists, but equally it may have arisen from students having already forgotten about lists issued five months previously. Whatever the answer may be, it does seem that, although the *majority* of undergraduates consider the guidance they receive about reading to be good, quite a substantial *minority* do not rate this guidance as good, do not rate the reading-lists as good (even when they *do* receive printed lists), and do not think that lecturers' advice on book-buying is good.

Of course students are critical people and it would be a miracle if they were all satisfied with their lecturers. Indeed it is a surprising fact that the *majority* of students seem to be reasonably satisfied with lecturers' guidance on the use of books.

But a great deal of the data on students' views of their lecturers' information is subjective and consists only of opinions. When we come to look at the factual data given by students about their own use of libraries and bookshops it can be asked if the students are not perhaps rather easily satisfied with the situation concerning books. Fifteen per cent of all students do not use a library for private study; 16 per cent do not borrow books from a library; 12 per cent spend no time in the week in a university library; 65 per cent had not used the Reserve-book Room during the past term; and 35 per cent had no books on loan from the university late in the Lent Term. Against this, a majority of students felt there were problems of obtaining books on loan for their work and a lack of multiple copies was noted, but overall only 18 per cent of all students felt that the university library stock in their subject was fairly or very poor. Only 9 per cent of students had ever used the line of communication from themselves to the lecturer to suggest a book which they felt ought to be in the library, and 47 per cent had no suggestions to offer for the improvement of the library service.

So it seems reasonable to conclude from these data that there is no great dissatisfaction amongst students about the library and the service it provides. But then those students who do not use the library either for study or borrowing might be assumed to have no need of it for their courses.

One explanation for a lack of need for library resources could be that students have sufficient books of their own for their studies. The questions on book-purchasing hardly support this hypothesis, since the average expenditure per student was

£16.80 for the year, and nearly 40 per cent of students had spent less than £12. Such sums of money do not purchase many books in these days, especially when so many educational textbooks are priced at £4 or over. Also 37 per cent of students had never ordered a book not in stock, which indicates a restricted enthusiasm for obtaining books, when so many students criticized the stocks of the two university bookshops.

Overall, then, the general picture seems to be of undergraduates perfectly able to pursue their courses of study with many of them making a distinctly limited use of books and yet not apparently feeling any great deprivation or worry about failing their courses. Failure rates do vary between subjects and faculties, but judging from the negative indicator of silence on this matter there is no problem of high failure rates in the university as a whole. Students pass their examinations in reasonable numbers and when, in the summer of 1973, one student out of thirty-three in the single school of sociology failed his final examination, this was discussed as a matter for concern at the subsequent staff meeting.

However, the discussion up to this point has been only in *general* terms and no mention has been made of *subject* differences, which have been shown in the survey tables to be most interesting and enlightening.

On books in particular

I have already, in earlier chapters, put forward tentative hypotheses about differences between various courses of study in the university and the effects that these have on the use of books. It is now a suitable point at which to offer a more general comment derived from the whole of the research project, which involved informal discussions with staff and students as well as the more formal survey.

Table 6.2 gave the different hours spent in classes for the eight faculties of the university and this table alone demonstrated how very different are the forms of instruction used in arts subjects as against technology subjects. I have already made a distinction between 'doing' subjects and 'reading' subjects, and this I believe is a crucial distinction for the understanding of the use of books. There is no simple continuum upon which one can place all the subjects taught in the university, but if I were forced to contrast two illustrative types of students I would select the historian and the mathematician. From answers given by students themselves one can construct archetypes which bring out the maximum contrasts.

The history student can be seen as a person whose whole subject is contained in books and, at university level, none of these can be considered as 'textbooks'. The history student must read and read and read so as to be aware of the contrasting views held by different historians and, whilst some authors may be more eminent than others, no one writer has the last word and no lecture course can be dependent upon one book. So the history student must be a great user of books, and outside his limited number of hours in class he must spend a great deal of time with books either bought, or borrowed from the library.

The undergraduate student of mathematics can be viewed as a person who is primarily concerned with learning and understanding extremely complicated processes of thought, which are very difficult to master but which must be mastered before he can proceed to the next stage. He is not so much concerned with people's views and opinions on what might be as with learning what has been established beyond reasonable doubt by mathematicians. So for this student the working-out of problems on the blackboard and note-pad is basic, and books are merely for reference if he finds himself unable to understand what occurred in the class. And even if he does turn to a book, he may find it valueless if the notation is different from that used by the lecturer. In examinations the mathematics student who can 'do' the questions set may gain 100 per cent marks (or even more in some cases), whereas, if he cannot 'do' the question, then no 'padding' or 'waffle' will help him, and a zero mark may be given. Historians (and certainly in my experience, sociologists) never get marks of 100 per cent, but equally are highly unlikely to get no marks at all.

In giving this contrast between the hypothetical historian and mathematician, I intend no value judgment as to which student is 'better' or 'worse' than the other. Both students will be strictly examined and their marks and degrees ratified by external examiners. Both will have benefited from three years of intellectual discipline at university. But their *forms* of study will have been different and their dependence on books will have differed.

It can thus be seen that, for example, students of civil engineering differ greatly from philosophers, language students from dental students, and law students from architects. All of them, in their various ways, are developing skills and knowledge, but in some cases the student is dealing with tangible matters which require him to spend many hours in laboratory, workshop or hospital. In other cases the subject matter is *words*, and so for the lawyer, the philosopher and the language student the book is the object of study and the thing to which many hours of study must be devoted. Of course, even these particular cases have exceptions, such is the variety of university work. Students of French, German and Spanish may spend time in the language laboratory developing their use of languages in addition to their understanding of literature. In the social sciences, students of geography will work on map and field projects, psychologists will carry out experiments in their laboratory, and sociologists will learn the practical skills of sampling and surveys. Diversity is the essence of the true university and from this diversity there arises the variety of dependence on books.

The implications of diversity

If it is accepted that the undergraduate need for books varies greatly between disciplines and courses, this does not mean that whatever is found to be the factual situation is necessarily the optimum or most functional. It may be that a professor or lecturer does not issue a duplicated reading-list to students or bookshop or even order new books for the library—and this situation may not have changed for many years. If it is so, then the professor or lecturer is not using the communication system at all and there must be something wrong with the course he is giving.

In a slightly different way, the lecturer may give detailed reading-lists to his students but omit to give the same information to the library or bookshop, in which case the students will be frustrated in their efforts to borrow or buy.

No matter how the actual course given by the lecturer may be taught, if there *is* a need for books, then students, librarians and bookshops all need to be kept informed. No one group of the four concerned—lecturers, students, librarians and booksellers—can operate efficiently without all four of them being brought together in the communication network. It does not matter if the course is in technology and leans heavily on a few carefully chosen texts, or if it is in politics or sociology and uses a long list of undifferentiated books: the principle of communication between the four groups remains important.

In focusing this research on the student, the prime user of the books, I have concentrated on student communications with lecturers, libraries and bookshops. I know from many discussions over the period of the research that librarians wish for better communications with teaching staff, as do the booksellers. Relationships between librarians and booksellers must not be overlooked, but I have the impression that, as they have a professional and business basis, these are reasonably good.

Universities, however, are not always very business-like places. Authority and responsibility are not always easy to pin down. Committees can meet many times and come to no decisions. And, above all, university teaching staff hold firmly to the right to teach their own courses in their own way. It is to be hoped that this right will not be undermined as universities become even larger and even more bureaucratic. But if the lecturers are to defend their freedom to teach as they will, they must look to their responsibilities to their students and other colleagues—among whom librarians are an important group and among whom booksellers deserve to be included.

Emerson once wrote ' 'Tis the good reader that makes the good book.' It is clear from the research in this book and in other surveys that many undergraduates are not good readers and thus do not make optimum use of the library facilities provided for them. Library policy in the past has tended to concentrate attention on the books rather than on the readers. Only in recent years has the *educational* function of the library staff come to be recognized and reader-service librarians and tutor librarians appointed.

Gradually it is being realized that libraries are complicated and even awe-inspiring institutions for young and inexperienced readers, and detailed courses of *subject* instruction are beginning to be provided. But in many cases ideas for undergraduate instruction thought up by librarians are coldly received by lecturing staff, who still do not appreciate how much better students would be were they able to use more skilfully the library facilities that already exist. Of course, many teaching staff are themselves unskilled in library use, and it is surprising how many of one's colleagues rarely seem ever to be in the library themselves. The network link between lecturers, librarians and students is an important one for the students, but it does require prior education of the lecturing staff by librarians.

Booksellers, those 'generous, liberal-minded men' as Johnson called them, have a special position in the network, since they must earn their livings by their efforts and there are no University Grants Committee or Department of Education and Science grants for them. The bookseller must operate by skilful persuasion and straightforward business efficiency. His major need, in order to attain his end of providing service to the university, is for information. Unfortunately some academic staff do not recognize their own responsibilities to booksellers and do not see that to deprive the bookseller of information is to deprive the students of books. There is antagonism to booksellers from some academics who are opposed to all forms of capitalistic enterprise, but probably the major problem is that of thoughtlessness and apathy. Since pressure from heads of departments is often very weak, perhaps this could be a useful cause for militant students to take up, since they are the ultimate victims.

It might be thought that a grand solution to the problem of communication would be to set up a committee which included representatives of the teaching staff, the library, the bookshops and the students. Theoretically this sounds very attractive but attendance at such committees is not always so good as it might be, and student participation quickly drops off when such representation is given to them. No committee can replace the genuinely human and personal contact which is needed when people talk to each other about books. The tragedy is that, as universities become bigger and bigger, the contact between people as individuals becomes so much more difficult.

Appendix I

Details of Bookshop Correspondent Scheme

The proposed scheme

It is proposed that in all departments there should be a Departmental Bookshop Correspondent responsible for co-ordinating detailed information about the books prescribed and recommended (for purchase) for courses to be held in the department. The information would be entered on standard forms, each accommodating six individual items (see example at the end of this appendix), which could be readily separated and filed by the bookshops. The forms would be supplied in a pad, so that a carbon copy could be retained by the department. In the regular annual return, the departmental list (consisting normally of a sheaf of forms) would be sent to the Deputy Librarian, who would immediately pass Xerox copies to the two bookshops. The bookshops have agreed to make financial contributions to cover costs. Any subsequent enquiries about a department's returns would be a matter of direct communication between the Departmental Correspondent and the bookshops. The responsibilities of the Departmental Bookshop Correspondent would fall mainly towards the end of a session, at the time when the courses for the following session have been decided; he would be asked to make his returns in the period between mid-June and mid-July. If, however, any new items were to be added to the purchase-lists at any time during a session, he would follow the same procedure. The Correspondent would naturally maintain close contact with the Head of the Department; he would keep in touch with the bookshops, and would transmit to lecturers any information relevant to the books recommended for their courses. He would be asked from time to time by the Standing Committee on Bookshops Facilities to submit to it a report on the working of the scheme and the response of the bookshops, and to include in it any complaints of substance. His responsibilities could, if desired, be combined with those of Departmental Library Correspondent. It is hoped that the practice, recently adopted by some departments, of sending complete *reading*-lists (as opposed to purchase-lists) to the library for information may be extended, and that the Correspondent will send three copies of such lists, so that two can be forwarded to the bookshops for their information and guidance.

The bookshops have undertaken

   i   to ensure that between them the total stocking position of each item is satisfactory;

  ii   to provide Departmental Bookshops Correspondents, at the beginning of a session, with information covering the number of books ordered and the number held in stock;

 iii   to inform Departmental Correspondents in good time of any items which are unavailable or are subject to shortage or delay.

The scheme is an attempt to provide a simple co-ordinated procedure, enabling all information to reach the bookshops, swiftly and at the right time, through a single channel which the library, with its resources and experience, can most appropriately provide. The Committee believes that if this scheme were adopted and fully implemented, the university would have created a situation in which the bookshops could be expected to give their best service. It must be emphasized that the scheme can only work effectively if it is accepted and implemented by all departments.

The Committee therefore *recommends:*

a   that the scheme as described above, be put into effect;

b   that a Departmental Bookshop Correspondent be appointed in every department, with the following duties:

   i   to co-ordinate the lists of books essential or recommended for purchase in connection with courses to be given in the department during the following session;

  ii   to transmit such lists, on standard forms, to the Deputy Librarian at the appropriate times;

 iii   to transmit to the Deputy Librarian three copies of any lists of recommended reading issued in the department;

iv   to maintain liaison with the Head of Department,
with his other departmental colleagues, and with the
two bookshops;

v   to report to the Standing Committee on Bookshop
Facilities when requested, on the working of the
scheme, including any complaints of substance.

c   that a full list of Departmental Bookshops Correspondents
be sent at the beginning of each session to the Deputy Librarian,
the booksellers, and to all Heads of Departments.

Notes for the guidance of Departmental Bookshop Correspondents
(Covering notes to accompany pad of bookshop information
forms)

General

1   This pad is designed to enable you to make recommendations to Sheffield booksellers to stock those books which the
staff of your department consider to be essential or strongly
recommended for student courses.

2   Each page of the pad is made up of six individual slips
on which separate books should be listed. Please fill in as
many slips as are needed and send the appropriate number of
pages back *to the Deputy Librarian* and *not* to bookshops.

3   The university library will have copies made of your
recommendations and these will be passed on as quickly as
possible to Bowes and Bowes, University Bookshop, Leavygreave, and to Hartley Seed, West Street.

4   Please note that recommendations to the bookshops
should be restricted to books which staff consider to be either
essential for purchase or strongly recommended for purchase.
Please do not include any books not in either of these
categories.

Completing the forms

1   Please collect the information about books for courses
from your colleagues in whatever way you deem most
convenient, but please will *you* send the *complete set* of
sheets to the Deputy Librarian.

2   The request from the library for your bookshop recom-

mendations is sent out in mid-June and your reply is needed *not later* than mid-July if the booksellers are to have books in stock for October. Please help by making your return as soon as possible.

3 It must be expected that some staff will be more co-operative than others. Please do not delay your reply beyond mid-July if your Departmental colleagues have not all given you their recommendations—the booksellers will do their best with any later recommendations, but they *must* have the bulk of them by mid-July at the latest.

Example of the form used by Bookshop Correspondents

Each page of the pad contains six of these forms.

UNIVERSITY OF SHEFFIELD BOOKSHOP INFORMATION FORM	DEPARTMENT	DATE / / 19

AUTHOR (Surname First) .... ☐ E

TITLE (If a particular Edition is required please specify) ☐ R

....

....

PUBLISHER (If known)

NUMBER OF STUDENTS ON COURSE ☐   YEAR OF COURSE ☐   FOR LIBRARY USE

NAME OF MEMBER OF STAFF GIVING COURSE ....

Other matters

1 If, at any time in the year, you or your colleagues wish to let the booksellers know of essential or recommended books, please send a page of the pad to the Deputy Librarian. This will apply, for example, in the case of special books for the Lent Term or newly published books.

2 The library and the booksellers derive great benefit from

knowing about books recommended for student *reading* (not necessarily for purchase). If you can let the Deputy Librarian have *three copies* of reading-lists issued in your department this will be valuable supplementary information.

Appendix II

Survey questionnaire*

Sheffield University use of books survey

1 Guidance from lecturers

1 **In general** do you think the guidance about reading which you receive from the lecturers on your course is
Very good ☐ Fairly good ☐ So-so ☐ Poor ☐ Very poor ☐

2 **In general** do you receive printed (duplicated) reading lists for the courses you take?
All ☐ Most ☐ Some ☐ Few ☐ None ☐

3 **In general** do you think the reading lists you do receive are
Very good ☐ Good ☐ So-so ☐ Poor ☐ Very poor ☐

4 How many lecture courses are you taking this year?
. . . . courses.

5 Are there any courses for which you think the guidance about reading is inadequate?
Yes ☐ No ☐
IF YES, how many courses?   . . . . courses.

6 Are there any courses for which you do not receive any printed (duplicated) reading lists?
Yes ☐ No ☐
IF YES, how many courses?   . . . . courses.

7 Do you receive guidance from your lecturers about what books to **buy**?
All ☐ Most ☐ Some ☐ Few ☐ None ☐

8 Do you consider the guidance on what books to **buy** is
Very good ☐ Good ☐ So-so ☐ Poor ☐ Very poor ☐

9 Please give any comments on the guidance you get from lecturers on reading and book buying which you feel would be helpful.
. . . .
. . . .

* This questionnaire was printed on A4 paper for the survey.

2   Use of the library

Please note that there are over 30 libraries in the University, including all departmental libraries. The 'main library' referred to below is the principal university library by the Arts Tower.

1   Which library do you use most for private study?
Name.................................   None used ☐

2   Which library do you use most for borrowing books?
Name.................................   None used ☐

3   How many hours a week are you normally in classes of any sort?   .... hours.

4   Excluding hall libraries, about how many hours a week do you usually spend in a university library? .... hours.

5   So far this **term** (since Christmas) how many times have you used a book in the main library Reserve Book Room?
.... times.

6   How many university library books have you out now?
.... books.

7   Do you have difficulty in getting books in the library for essays or projects for your courses?
Very much ☐ Fairly much ☐ So-so ☐ Not much ☐
None at all ☐

8   Do you have any difficulty because of lack of multiple copies of particular books?
Very much ☐ Fairly much ☐ So-so ☐ Not much ☐
None at all ☐

9   **In general** do you consider the university library stock in your subject(s) is
Very good ☐ Fairly good ☐ So-so ☐ Fairly poor ☐
Very poor ☐

10 Have you ever suggested to a lecturer a book that you think ought to be in the library?
Yes ☐ No ☐

11 Please give any suggestions for the improvement of the university library service.
....
....
....

3   Sheffield bookshops

The following questions refer mainly to the two bookshops which stock university books—A. B. Ward's of Leavygreave and Hartley Seed's of West Street.

1   Which bookshop do you normally buy your course books from?
Ward's ☐ Hartley Seed's ☐ Neither ☐
If neither please say what shop, if any, you use
. . . .

2   Do you think the stock in your subject(s) of the two Sheffield shops is

Ward's   Very good ☐   Good ☐   So-so ☐   Poor ☐
Very poor ☐   Don't know ☐
Hartley Seed's   Very good ☐   Good ☐   So-so ☐   Poor ☐
Very poor ☐   Don't know ☐

3   At the shop you ticked in Question 1 have you ever ordered a book not in stock?
Yes ☐ No ☐
IF YES, (*a*) about how many books altogether have you ordered?   . . . . books.
(*b*) In general was delivery Very quick ☐ Fairly quick ☐ So-so ☐ Fairly slow ☐ Very slow ☐
(*c*) Can you give a time for your fastest delivery?
. . . .
(*d*) Can you name any books you have had to wait a long time for on order?
. . . .
. . . .

4   At the shop ticked in Question 1, do you find the staff Very helpful ☐   Fairly helpful ☐   So-so ☐   Fairly unhelpful ☐   Very unhelpful ☐

5   About how much money do you reckon you have spent on books for study this session (i.e. 1971–72 academic year)?
£ . . . .

6   Allowing for differences between hard-cover and paperback editions do you think in **general** that the prices of books in your subject(s) are

Very high ☐   Fairly high ☐   So-so ☐   Fairly low ☐
Very low ☐
7   Can you give any examples of books you have bought which you consider to be very expensive?
....
....
8   Please give any suggestions for improving the service of the university bookshops.
....
....
....

4   About yourself

These details are needed only for analysing the important differences between different years and different courses. No individual examples will be used in the analysis.

1   What faculty are you in? ....
2   What course of study are you taking? ....
3   What year of study are you in? ....
4   If you are a first year student taking a faculty rather than a departmental course (e.g. three Arts or Social Sciences) please give the subjects being taken.
....
5   If you are a second or third year student on a general, dual or triple degree, please give the subjects being taken.
....
6   Do you live in hall ☐   lodgings ☐   flat or similar ☐ at home ☐?
7   The full undergraduate grant is now £430 a year (or £345 for home students) plus academic fees and union fees paid direct. Do you receive
Full grant ☐   More than half ☐   Less than half ☐   The minimum ☐
8   Are you single ☐ or married ☐?
9   Are you male ☐ or female ☐?

THANK YOU VERY MUCH

Now please put this questionnaire in the envelope provided and return it for analysis.

Notes

Chapter 1   The theoretical problem

1 University Grants Committee, *Report of the Committee on Libraries* (Parry Report) (HMSO, London, 1967).
2 Harry Fairhurst, 'The book needs and book-buying habits of undergraduates', *Bookselling News*, vol. 6, no. 11 (November 1970).
3 A standard code of three stars, two stars and one star for recommendations to indicate—*** = Essential purchase by all students; ** = Strongly recommended for purchase; and * = Recommended reading—was advocated in a trade pamphlet 'Improving communication and service in academic bookselling', published in 1973 by the College and University Booksellers' Group of the Booksellers' Association of Great Britain.
4 The original statement was probably Carlyle's view that 'The true university of these days is a collection of books.'
5 Parry Report, p. 4.
6 See ibid. for statement on the functions of libraries.
7 For an excellent discussion of this theme see the inaugural lecture of Professor W. L. Saunders, 'Humanistic institution or information factory?', *Journal of Librarianship*, vol. 1, no. 4 (October 1969).
8 Peter Stockham, *University Bookselling* (Hutchinson, London, 1965) (*Better Bookselling*: Pamphlet No. 1).
9 Since writing this I have heard of some academic publishers withdrawing this field force.
10 See 'The bookshop and the book buyer', ch. 3 of Peter H. Mann, *Books: Buyers and Borrowers* (André Deutsch, London, 1971).
11 See Peter H. Mann, 'Bookselling: an occupational survey' (University of Sheffield, Department of Sociological Studies, November 1971).

Chapter 2   University libraries and bookshops

1 Parry Report, p. 4.
2 Ibid.
3 Ibid., p. 1.
4 A project sponsored by the Department of Education and Science, directed by Professor W. L. Saunders, with Mr T. D. Wilson as principal investigator.
5 L. Jolley, 'The function of the university library', *Journal of Documentation*, vol. 18, no. 3 (September 1962), p. 134.
6 Bruce Truscot's *Red Brick University* was published in 1943, and *Red Brick and these Vital Days* was published in 1945.

The two were published as one book *Red Brick University*
by Penguin, Harmondsworth in 1951. It is a pity that
Bruce Truscot (who was a professor at Liverpool) is no longer
read; he should be compulsory reading for all trendy new
academics.

7 Jolley, op. cit., p. 134.
8 'Report of the Committee on Australian Universities'
   (Murray Committee) (Canberra, 1957).
9 Parry Report, p. 9.
10 Jolley, op. cit., p. 136.
11 Both quoted in Saunders, 'Humanistic institution or information
    factory?', *Journal of Librarianship*, vol. 1, no. 4 (October 1969),
    p. 200.
12 Ibid., p. 198.
13 Ibid., p. 199.
14 Ibid., p. 201.
15 See *The Times Higher Education Supplement* (18 August 1972),
    p. 5 for table, p. 8 for editorial, and p. 1 for Mr Thompson's
    comments.
16 L. Jolley, 'University of Western Australia: report on the library
    for the year 1969', n.p. (annual report to the library).
17 Parry Report, p. 63.
18 Ibid., p. 46.
19 Jolley, 'The function of the university library', pp. 139–40.
20 Jolley, 'University of Western Australia: report on the library'.
21 Maurice B. Line, 'Student attitudes to the University Library:
    a survey at Southampton University', *Journal of Documentation*,
    vol. 19, no. 3 (September 1963), p. 105.
22 T. H. Bowyer, 'Considerations on book provision for
    undergraduates in British university libraries', *Journal of
    Documentation*, vol. 19, no. 4 (December 1963), p. 165.
23 Parry Report, p. 41.
24 Ibid., p. 44.
25 Ibid., pp. 66–7.
26 Jolley, 'University of Western Australia: report on the library'.
27 Parry Report, p. 11.
28 K. W. Humphreys, 'Survey of borrowing from the Main Library,
    the University of Birmingham', *Libri*, vol. 14 (1964), p. 137.
29 P. E. Tucker, 'The sources of books for undergraduates:
    a survey at Leeds University Library', *Journal of Documentation*,
    vol. 17, no. 2 (June 1961), p. 92.
30 Bowyer, op. cit., p. 157.
31 B. S. Page and P. E. Tucker, 'The Nuffield pilot survey of
    library use in the University of Leeds', *Journal of Documentation*,
    vol. 15, no. 1 (March 1959), p. 6.
32 Parry Report, p. 187.
33 Ibid., p. 195.
34 Ibid., pp. 193–4.
35 Ibid., p. 195.

36 Ibid., p. 193.
37 Ibid., p. 188.
38 Ibid., pp. 196–8.
39 P. Durey, 'A survey of student library-use at the University of Keele', *Research in Librarianship*, vol. 2, no. 7 (January 1968), p. 6.
40 Parry Report, p. 187.
41 Report by Birmingham University Library on surveys carried out in 1964 on the use of the library by undergraduates, graduate students and staff (Appendix 5 to the Parry Report).
42 Tucker, op. cit., p. 82.
43 Durey, op. cit., p. 4.
44 Tucker, op. cit., p. 84.
45 Parry Report, p. 19.
46 Line, op. cit., p. 115.
47 Tucker, op. cit., p. 87.
48 Ibid., p. 90.
49 Line, op. cit., p. 104.
50 Maurice B. Line, 'The college student and the library' (University of Southampton Institute of Education, 1965).
51 Ibid., p. 21.
52 Line, 'Student attitudes to the University Library', pp. 111–12.
53 Ibid., p. 114.
54 Parry Report, p. 187.
55 Jolley, 'Function of the university library', pp. 138–9.
56 Line, 'The college student and the library', p. 19.
57 Saunders, op. cit., p. 207.
58 'Grants to students', Department of Education and Science (revised 1971).
59 Parry Report, p. 42.
60 Stockham, *University Bookselling*, p. 10.
61 For details of pay see Mann, 'Bookselling; an occupational survey' (University of Sheffield, Department of Sociological Studies, November 1971).
62 Julian Blackwell, 'Some problems of bookselling', *ASLIB Proceedings*, vol. 14, no. 3 (March 1962), pp. 57–62.
63 Stockham, op. cit., p. 22.
64 Ibid., p. 33.
65 Julian Blackwell, 'Bookselling to universities', *Journal of Documentation*, vol. 20, no. 4 (December 1964), p. 193.
66 Parry Report, pp. 39–40.
67 Ibid., p. 41.
68 Stockham, op. cit., p. 35.
69 Parry Report, p. 39.
70 Tucker, op. cit., p. 90.
71 Line, 'The college student and the library', pp. 46–7.
72 Line, 'Student attitudes to the University Library', p. 106.
73 Parry Report, p. 199.
74 'Study of book buying and reading habits of the college student

and the college professor', conducted for the Association of
American Publishers Inc. (College Division) by Gilbert Youth
Research Inc. (February 1972).
75 Bowyer, op. cit., p. 153.
76 See Parry Report pp. 39–41 for discussion of this topic.
77 Ibid., p. 42.

Chapter 3   Sheffield University and books
1 The data are all taken from 'Annual reports to the Court',
   University of Sheffield.
2 Library data are also taken from 'Annual reports to the Court'.
3 W. L. Saunders, E. W. Roberts and L. J. Wickison, 'Survey of
   borrowing from the University of Sheffield Library during
   one academic year' in W. L. Saunders (ed.), *The Provision and
   Use of Library and Documentation Services* (Pergamon, Oxford,
   1966).
4 'Survey 1961', University of Sheffield Union of Students (March
   1961).
5 'Memorandum to the University Grants Committee',
   University of Sheffield Union of Students (January 1966), pp. 34–5.
6 Trevor Noble and Bridget Pym, 'Collegial authority and the
   receding locus of power', *British Journal of Sociology*, vol. 21,
   no. 4 (December 1970).
7 See Appendix I for full Bookshop Correspondents' details.

Index